1

"The fields were my theatre"

Written by Trevor Weeks MBE

Editorial Thanks to Dilly Barlow and Kathy Martyn

The book has been written to raise vital funds for East Sussex Wildlife Rescue & Ambulance Service , Reg Charity 1108880. www.wildlifeambulance.org.

East Sussex WRAS, PO Box 2148, Seaford, East Sussex, BN25 9DE.

www.facebook.com/wildlifeambulance

Cover Design By: Steve Jones mpasfphotography.com

Published by:

Trevor Weeks MBE

East Sussex WRAS, Unit 8 The Shaw Barn, Whitesmith, East Sussex, BN8 6JD

ISBN: 978-0-9933753-0-9

Printed and bound in Great Britain by Clays Ltd, St Ives plc

Thank you to all our supporters!

"30 years ago I was just a young lad of 13 who loved nature and the environment. I saw first-hand how our wildlife suffered because there were too few people out there able to help. Slowly over the years I have managed to build from being a one man band to a registered charity with four ambulances and our Casualty Care Centre with three registered vets! Many people look at me as the person who has achieved this, but WRAS is much bigger than just me. These wild animals and birds would still be dying slow and painful deaths if it wasn't for people like you helping and volunteering.

Thank you to everyone who has helped support me over the years, helped teach me new skills and given me the opportunity to gain new experiences.

My biggest thanks goes to our supporters who make regular donations or standing orders with us, this has really helped to make us secure and enabled us to push forward in the way we have.

Thank you for helping to make my childhood dream come true, and for all the hard work you have put in helping our local wildlife and preventing suffering. You are the true heroes!

Thank you to everyone who has helped produce this book and those who have made me the person I am today. Mum, I hope you are proud of me."

Trevor Weeks MBE founder of East Sussex WRAS.

Chapter 1 - The Fields Were My Theatre.

I used to think that people in their forties were old! My hair's going grey, my beard is looking more like a badger every day, and I've now been undertaking wildlife rescue and conservation work for over 30 years. Going to Buckingham Palace to pick up an MBE for services to animal welfare still feels like a dream - did that really happen?

I was born in January 1972 in Eastbourne, about two months premature. Some people say this was because I couldn't wait to start my wild life!

I don't remember a time when animals haven't been present in my life. My parents both spent time working on farms and we had all sorts of pets at home while I was growing up. I have to admit that as a young child, my early encounters with small creatures weren't brilliant. Why do kids try to eat worms?

I remember watching friends drop ants onto the hotplate of an old Raeburn stove and watching them explode, and although I laughed at the time, it didn't sit comfortably with me. A far better and more honourable encounter with ants was when I went out walking in the woods. I discovered that if you dropped a bluebell flower onto an ants' nest, it would turn pink. It was fascinating. It was only later, when studying science at school that I learnt that the change from blue to pink is similar to the litmus test for acidity. Blue litmus paper turns red under acidic conditions and red litmus paper turns blue under alkaline. The bluebell is an anthocyanin which is a water-soluble pigment that changes colour when exposed to acids. As the ants attack the invading bluebell, they bite it injecting formic acid into the bluebell and the petals change to pink.

We had a black cat called Kim that had been rescued from a farm at Ovingdean where my grandfather worked. From what I remember my mum telling me, Kim had been cornered and picked on by some of the farm dogs, and after being nursed back to health, she came and lived with us at our family home in Hailsham. Kim was not a lap-cat; she enjoyed her independence too much for that. She knew we welcomed her, that she had a family, but preferred to do her own thing.

We also had a large white rabbit, a black guinea pig, some chickens, a pond and an aquarium full of fish, tanks with stick insects, and at one point even a terrapin. My mum would send my older brother and I out to the privet hedge to pick small twigs and leaves to go inside the stick insects' little containers. It was all the craze back in the 1970s, a bit like the Ninja turtle craze in the 1980s.

One creature that made a huge impact on me was our dog Sam, a black greyhound cross. She was from the Raystede Centre for Animal Welfare, at Ringmer. We visited her at the beginning of 1979. She was the only dog that came up to see us when we walked round and she clearly wanted to come home with us. It was shortly after my seventh birthday that we went to collect her. As one of the volunteers walked her across the car park, she slipped her lead, ran up to us and jumped onto the bonnet of our old Austin 1100 car. How she knew that was our car I have no idea.

Back home she proved to be a wonderful pet. My mum took her for walks in the woods every day for a couple of hours at a time, and often my brother and I would tag along. She loved playing with us and I remember the tight feeling in my chest from laughing so hard when she used to grab our trouser legs and pull us round the kitchen floor. In the field behind our home my parents would hold onto Sam while my brother and I ran off up the field. We would call her, and as soon as they released her, she would sprint off after us often knocking us to the floor like skittles. Afterwards we would collapse on the sofa and she would stretch herself out next to us.

She was very much a family dog and when relatives came over, we would often walk across to the woods. We would split into two chatting groups, with Sam constantly running between us trying to round us up like sheep to keep us all together.

These walks into the countryside really helped me to appreciate my surroundings and the value of nature, although I don't think I realised this at the time. It was only when I grew older, and started to see more and more areas where I used to play being bulldozed and covered in concrete, that I fully appreciated how lucky I had been, and how today many young people miss out.

All the local families used to go blackberry picking, either in the woods or often up at the old station yard in Hailsham, now Lindfield Drive. Being so young I don't remember too much of the site, but I can remember climbing into the old engine shed and being scared as it was so derelict. We used to run along the disused

platforms and trying to balance on the remaining bits of track, rather more fun than helping to pick blackberries. My mum was a fantastic cook and always baking. She turned the blackberries into delicious jams, jellies, crumbles, pies and more. She insisted on attempting to get me to eat tomatoes, parsnips, prunes and rhubarb, despite me hating them. She would cut the parsnips into the same shapes as the roast potatoes, trying to fool us into eating them. Disgusting vegetables!

My father's parents lived in the hamlet known as Berwick Station, about a mile north of Berwick Village. We were often there at weekends which also gave me a great opportunity to explore the countryside. Berwick Station had two brickyards, the Cuckmere and Ludlay. Both had been closed down not long after the war. They were very overgrown and we would sneak off to explore, using our wild imaginations to turn them into camps and dragon's dens. We used to dare each other to enter the drying tunnels. They were so dark you couldn't see anything, and we would scare each other by talking about ghosts, and end up running out screaming if something touched us.

One of the yards slightly further away was also very scary but equally as enticing, with lots of old machinery and equipment. There were sheds full of pulleys, large fan belts, and old rusting machinery. The tracks and trolleys were still there, which we used to push around. I so wish I had been just a few years older to have appreciated and remembered it better. I'm sure modern health and safety would have something to say these days if children were running around such sites. But back then, if you got injured, your parents were likely to slap you round the head and tell you off for doing whatever it was that caused you to have an accident. At least it taught you the hard way not to do it again.

I was (and still am) rather accident prone, and when young, very clumsy. My left thumb has a damaged nail. I don't remember how I damaged it but from what I have been told a couple of bits of metal became embedded in my thumb from a hinged blackboard. I still bear the scars both sides of my thumb and my nail has never grown back properly since. But however it happened it was undoubtedly a case of me doing something I shouldn't.

A few times on my way to school half asleep, I walked right into lamp posts. There is an old footpath railway bridge which crosses from Downsview Way in Hailsham to where White House Primary School used to be in North Street - what is now a supermarket. The approach used to be steeper than it is now, and in the ice and snow, I was always the one who slipped up and fell over.

When the fields at the back of our house in South Road were built on, we used to play there. Being a building site there were all sorts of hazards such as nails sticking up through wood. Inevitably I was the one who stepped on them and twice ended up visiting hospital. Even when playing at the bottom of our relatively safe garden I managed to put a garden fork through my brother's foot.

In retrospect I think that most of these "accidents" were born out of an innate curiosity about how things worked and a short attention span. In the infants at Whitehouse Primary School I was forever being told off for not paying attention. I was fascinated by patterns, puzzles and finding out how things worked which often resulted in me breaking them or pressing buttons that I shouldn't have. I loved constructing things out of Lego bricks. I was a bit disorganised in my approach scattering everything about and concentrating on the end result, and constantly being told off by my mum for losing or leaving bits lying around. Looking back I can see how I used to divide the blocks up into groups, trying to make logical patterns or design things like a young inventor. My parents gave me Meccano sets and I would always find I never had enough bits for what I was trying to build and construct. This was probably where my interest in logic and problem solving came from and in fact proved to be very useful later in life as I moved into computer programming and management.

But no matter how much trouble I landed myself in or how many minor injuries I inflicted on myself, none of this deterred me from enthusiastically pulling things apart to see how they worked, or exploring the countryside or derelict sites such as the old brickyards. They may have held hazards for an accident-prone boy, but they were also a haven for wildlife. Watching a barn owl one summer evening enthralled me, and I got a severe reprimand for not being home on time.

The banks around the brickyards used to be covered in primroses. Every year there would be an amazing display, and my Nan would pick them for the local church, making up large basketfuls.

Arlington Reservoir was just up the road. I would walk up there with a few slices of bread and feed the ducks. It took me a while before I dared walk all the way round the reservoir, but once I was old enough it became a real delight, and a walk I still do from time to time. The old metal bridge, which crossed the River Cuckmere from the edge of the reservoir to Arlington Church, used to scare me, and on one walk I was so frightened that I refused to cross it - much to the annoyance of my parents.

I am so grateful to my parents for the trips we went on and our outings to the countryside. We didn't go far, but as a child it seemed it at the time. We once had a picnic in a recently cut corn field between Beddingham and Lewes, close to where the level crossing once was. We sat behind a large circular hay bale, had a picnic on a blanket and waved to the trains as they went past.

We would drive to the top of Bo-Beep, the hill behind Alciston, for picnics and to appreciate the view. The whole family decided to take a walk up to the top of Mount Caburn at Glynde, equipped with our first proper pair of binoculars with an amazing X10 zoom. The ancient hill fort was a fascinating place with splendid panoramic views. I spent ages looking through the binoculars watching people, trains, cars, birds, cows in the fields and much more.

At harvest time all the local children from the surrounding roads would gather in the fields to rake up the cut grass. We would stack it up to make eight feet high walls forming houses with corridors and rooms, but no roofs. In the woods we would cut "pugging sticks" - long flexible hazel or hornbeam shoots about four feet in length. We would then stick a small,

11

rolled up ball of clay on the end and, with a flick of the wrist, the ball of clay would fly off and travel some distance. We often had wars in the woods, and several times I ended up with round bruises on my face. The many streams in the wood provided endless hours of fun; trying to make dams and bridges; attempting to divert water or dismantling naturally forming dams to help the water flow properly. We revelled in these endless hours of entertainment out in the countryside, which many children and teenagers miss out on these days.

There used to be a car park in North Street Hailsham, now the car park for the Quintin's Centre. There was a large electronic map with buttons you pressed that would light up different locations to help people find places in the town. The pathway that led to the town centre was next to an old orchard, and as children we would climb over the wall and go scrumping. In other words, stealing the apples!

Walking in southern Hailsham was great and there were, and still are, numerous pathways running behind or through the housing estates, so you didn't have to walk along the roadsides to get to the town centre. One of these pathways used to bring us out by Hailsham Common Pond, and we would always stop and feed the ducks and geese.

Another pathway we frequented went behind the old Rope factory off South Road and along Diplocks Industrial Estate. A large part of this was just fields and there were once about seven small ponds, including where Avocet Way now is. A pathway ran down the side of the factory, and there was a pond which had various broken branches, planks of wood and rubbish from the estate dumped in it. We spent hours here, catching slow worms and great crested newts which back then were very common in ponds around the area.

The spring was always a magical time and the flowers, leaves and bird song were quite enchanting, something I didn't really appreciate until my teenage years. At the end of South Road, where it joins the A22, is a grass bank. My parents used to take me there to look for glow worms. Their little tiny glowing green tails enchanted me, and really did seem like magic. It was not uncommon to see twenty to thirty at a time, but these days if I find one a season I am lucky.

Once old enough, I used to cycle into the countryside along the many back lanes as far as Lewes and Battle, frequently stopping to investigate the landscape and views that are so abundant in this part of Sussex. I was enthralled. East Sussex really is a beautiful county.

Of course, whilst out and about, I wasn't at home to feed and clean the many pets we had, and was frequently told off for not doing so. But mum would always ensure they were sorted out and looked after. Secretly I think she used us as an excuse to get the pets. She clearly loved all animals and she must have passed those genes on to me.

Every so often we would go on family outings, be it a coach trip to Cheddar Gorge or camping up in Worcestershire where our great auntie and uncle lived in Pershore. On one of these camping trips, as we returned home in the evening, there were bats flying back and forth along the lane above our heads, and we started ducking to avoid being hit by them. It makes me smile looking at back at those times. We also found a dead bat on a tree stump which was sad but fascinating. It was the first time we had seen a bat close up. I'm still captivated by them now - beautiful creatures.

It was at primary school that I discovered I had a milk intolerance. Every day we had to drink a third of a pint in those small glass milk bottles. They would often have been left in the sun and tasted warm and horrible. I began to suffer from acute diarrhoea and was seen by numerous doctors. I remember one bonfire night being severely ill and collapsing at Hankham Bonfire Display. My father had to carry me back to the car assisted by a police officer. I was taken home, placed in the bath and showered down and the doctor called. Although I don't remember much about it, I do know I was in bed for several days and I was finally diagnosed as being lactose intolerant.

I was also growing more particular about what I ate. As I grew older my parents tried to get me to eat meat off the bone, and proper fish, but I always struggled with this. Something just didn't seem right. Give me a burger or something which had no resemblance to an animal and I would eat it. I couldn't even eat boneless chunks of KFC chicken covered in batter.

Not surprisingly, the older I got, the more vegetarian I became. This wasn't so much because I was aware of the animal welfare issues around farming, but because I just couldn't bring myself to eat anything resembling an animal. I don't think I made a conscious decision about this at any time, that's just how I was.

The last family pet we had was Fred, a black and white cat. Unlike our previous cat Kim, Fred was much more a family cat, and would show off and want attention. One Saturday morning I remember being woken by the sound of meowing. I got up and opened my bedroom door, and at the bottom of the stairs was Fred. He was panting, and it was clear that something was wrong with him. I couldn't get hold of my dad, so called our vets, but their emergency service on a Saturday was over at Hampden Park. I knew I had to do something quickly, so took a taxi. She had been run over, but had managed to make it back home. I left her with the vets and got my father to ring them when he got home from work. Sadly, Fred didn't make it. I felt awful and hopeless at not having been able to do anything to help.

I think that was when the first seeds were sown that were to lead me down the path of animal rescue. Fred was, after all, a domestic pet. The vet might have been able to save him if his injuries weren't so bad. But it was the fact that I could do nothing that made me feel so helpless and hopeless. I wanted to find out more about how I could help not just injured animals, but also the countryside that I had grown up in, for which I was developing a very deep affection.

Chapter 2 - My Early mid-life crisis!

I was thirteen when my mum handed me a leaflet about the Eastbourne Conservation Volunteers. She thought I might be interested in joining them. Soon my weekends were spent wherever the latest project was; repairing Dew Ponds up on the Downs at Eastbourne; woodland management at Bramble Grove near Michelham Priory or building gates and stiles on footpaths near Hartfield. Sometimes there were tasks involving a bonfire, and I always took along a packet of marshmallows to cook on the end of a stick, or occasionally we would wrap spuds in tin foil and bake them for lunch.

I loved doing these jobs as it took me to parts of the countryside most people wouldn't normally visit. I'm not sure my father was always too pleased though as he had to drive me to all sorts of locations around the area.

Throughout our teenage years, my brother and I experienced the normal problems and issues associated with being troublesome adolescents. We both suffered from bullying at Hailsham Secondary School. I had a lack of confidence, which had not been helped by my grandfather's preference for my brother, who was almost two years older than me. I can remember staying with my grandparents one weekend and my father had come across with our dog Sam. I had been given a bowl of crisps and I gave one to Sam. My grandfather was very put out about this and told me off saying, "The crisps were for you and not the dog". He threatened to take them away from me if I gave Sam another. I wasn't too happy about this and replied, "You gave them to me and I want to share them with Sam. If you don't like that then I'm more than happy to pack my bags and go home". Which I did!

Our mum was quite strict, and at the time she was working nights. The following morning I was really scared that I was going to get told off. There was an enclosed stairway in our house, and I sat at the bottom with the door closed for ages, as I was so worried. To my surprise, when I finally plucked up the courage to open the door, my mum was hysterical with laughter, and congratulated me for standing up to my grandfather.

I also joined the St John Ambulance Cadets. My brother had already been there for a while, and more and more often, as had happened with my teachers at school, I found them saying "If your brother can do it, why can't you?" But I stuck it out for a few years and otherwise enjoyed my time there. As a cadet I managed to achieve several certificates in various first aid subjects like bandaging and resuscitation. We had marching and drill competitions in the hall and often I would come first. Subconsciously I think all this made me feel more positive, gave me more confidence and also helped me realise how helping others made me feel better about myself.

As my brother and I got older and more costly to look after, my parents worried about finances and paying the mortgage. My mum held down a couple of part time jobs, and my father was employed by the council's highway services. They both worked hard and long hours to make ends meet. I remember feeling very privileged to go along with my father, one snowy winter night, on one of his gritting rounds. I don't think I had ever been so high up in a vehicle before. Watching my father it was clear he took great pride in his work.

I always tried to make my parents proud of me, but it was a difficult balance between work and play, a balance I often seemed to get wrong, and I would end up disappointing them. I had a tendency to go over the top when I did something well or felt confident about something, but this often turned what should have been a positive situation into a negative one, getting me into trouble on occasions.

In the 1980s I was in the cub scouts, and one of our duties was to make a cup of tea at unusual locations, in one instance at a police station. I worked really hard on helping to make the tea and handing it out. A photographer turned up from the local paper and told us to give a big smile to the camera. So I did as instructed and pulled a really big, over-the-top smile which made me look really stupid. When it was printed in the local paper my parents were rather embarrassed and not very happy.

One Sunday morning, it must have been either Mother's Day or my mum's birthday, I thought it would be a really good idea to try and make breakfast for her. So I got up early, went down stairs and tried to light the Raeburn oven. I couldn't find any matches and I had observed my parents lighting a fire in the Raeburn by setting alight to a piece of rolled up newspaper on the old style electric hob. I tried to do the same thing but rather than using several pieces of paper tightly rolled up I used just one. It exploded in flames burning a couple of fingers in the process. I decided to change my plan and went for cereal instead! For the first hour or so I kept quiet about my fingers, but it wasn't long before they really started to hurt and I burst into tears. I can't remember exactly how old I was, but still in primary school. I had to be carted off to hospital to have them looked at. Although my parents realised I had been trying to do a good thing, when I returned to school after the weekend with my fingers bandaged up, I was told to come to the front of the hall. The head mistress paraded me in front of everyone as an example of what happens when you play with fire. I know she was only using me to illustrate an important point, but I felt very humiliated and stupid.

Starting Secondary school worried me. My primary school had encountered numerous problems when louts from Hailsham Secondary School tried to terrorise us and resulted in several confrontations with teachers and the police having to be called. I had heard various rumours about bullying within the Secondary School that really concerned me especially as I was aware that my brother had experienced problems.

Some people are surprised when I say I am shy. I come out of myself when I feel secure in my environment and with the people around me, but I'm very shy when in unfamiliar situations or people I don't know. Moving to secondary school was quite stressful. It wasn't helped when my girlfriend from primary school ended up in a different class from me and telling me out of the blue "I can do better than you" and not having anything else to do with me.

I became quite depressed, partly because I was being bullied, and partly because of typical teenager/parent issues at home. I was also still a bit accident prone and clumsy, which seemed to put people off being friends with me. When playing sport, if anyone was going to hit the ball over the fence or onto the roof it had to be me. Even though this was unintentional, I always got a good ticking off. I never made any close friends at school and often found myself being the butt of jokes and pranks from both students and teachers.

I can remember one bully from my brother's class pinning me up against a tree and using my school tie to bind me to a tree trunk. I think my fellow class mates were as shocked and frightened as I was, as none of them dared move or say anything. The teacher's response was just to say, "Keep away from them, that way they can't bully you." I've always thought that a very stupid remark!

Although my mum was strict with us, she certainly came out with some wise words from time to time. In my first or second year at secondary school there were numerous teacher strikes taking place, and we often found our lessons being interrupted. The sixth and seventh form students decided to hold a sit-in at the school, and encouraged the rest of us to take part. I really wanted to participate, but was worried how my mum would react if I did. So I phoned home, explained the situation to her and said I wanted to join them. Her reply was simple and her words have stayed with me always, "It's your choice, but you must be prepared to pay the consequences. You are responsible for your actions." I think she clearly appreciated me asking. Sadly I never got a chance to get involved as we were stopped by the teachers from getting to where the sit-in took place.

I have very fond memories of my Aunty Mary and Uncle Joe, who lived just down the road from us. They were not our real aunt and uncle but they often used to babysit for us when we were very young. We used to pop down and see them from time to time to show off any project or school work we had done. They were always very encouraging. I was really unsure what direction to go in at school and what career path to take. I remember Joe very wisely saying, "If you don't learn something you will never be able to do it, but if you do, it can never be taken away from you. There is always something to learn and you should never stop learning."

He was great at giving advice and guidance without actually telling you what you should do. He certainly helped me make up my mind on several occasions. Sadly neither Mary nor Joe are with us any longer, but I will always remember them with fondness.

Although I was accident prone, clumsy and not very co-ordinated when playing with a ball, there were some sports I found I was good at.

To help me cope with the bullying, my mum thought I might be interested in joining a new Judo club which had just started at the Summerheath Hall in Hailsham. This was a turning point for me as I found myself doing well and entering competitions. Several people I knew from school joined too, including some of the bullies, and I found myself being able to fight them legitimately and, more often than not, winning too. This helped reduce the bullying, build my confidence and my independence.

I had also become quite a good runner, more by accident than design. During my final year at primary school, our class had been to stay in a farmhouse in France. In the evening we found it hard to get to sleep, so one of the teachers would take us for a run round the village to tire us out and help us fall asleep quickly. The first night virtually everyone went for a run, but by the end of the stay it was just three of us. On my return home my mum suggested that I entered the Hailsham Fun Run. It was a nine mile run, and for five years in a row I entered. Each year my time got quicker and quicker. Then, in the local paper, I noticed details of the Beachy Head Marathon. I really fancied giving it a go, but was not old enough to enter on my own. So I wrote out a note and asked one of the teachers if they would display it on the teachers' staff-room notice board. A few days later, my French teacher agreed to enter with me and we also recruited four other students to train and enter. We did several long walks and practices before the event, that was taking place in February. The twenty six mile walk began at the start of the South Downs Way, went up the hill, across the top of Eastbourne to Jevington, then to Alfriston, along to Bo-Beep Hill above Alciston, round to the back of Seaford and back to the Cuckmere Valley. Then over to Litlington, down to Exceat, and up and along the Seven Sisters cliffs to Birling Gap, over Beachy Head and finally back down to where we started.

The first year I did this it had been snowing and there were deep snow drifts on the top of the Downs. But the speed at which we were walking helped us to keep warm. The end of the Marathon is a killer; you have to go up and down the Seven Sisters hills. It really makes your legs ache. The final check point was at Birling Gap and by then I was struggling. But I kept going, one foot in front of the other. I am still not sure how I got to the end, but I made it down the final hill to the finish line where I was awarded up my finishing medal. I was exhausted but really chuffed. For the next 4 days I could hardly walk, my legs were so stiff and ached so much that I ended up having to take time off school.

I did the Beachy Head marathon four more times, as well as the Rottingdean Windmill Marathon and the Brighton to Eastbourne Two Piers Walking Marathon. The first time I took part in the latter, I came second in the junior section. I would have come first if the winner had not run for part of the journey. As a walking race that was not allowed!

I raised money during each race for various organisations including the RSPCA, Stoke Mandeville Hospital, RNLI and Guide Dogs for the Blind.

As well as running marathons, and trying to study at school, I was also working. My parents had made me take on several paper rounds, and every Sunday morning I worked at a mushroom farm. I was paid about £3 for a morning's work. We picked mushrooms in long sheds, in dark damp conditions. Although I didn't mind the work, a couple of the people I had to work with were pretty unpleasant. One of the guys was constantly making sexist jokes and rude gestures that made me feel very uncomfortable. He would also often spit as he spoke. I stayed there for as long as I could, but after a while I stopped going.

Around this time several things happened that were to have a profound effect on me, both emotionally and philosophically. I read a book and saw three films. These were to change my outlook on life and my attitude to the world and what went on in it.

The book was called "Sussex After the Bomb - What Will Happen to Newhaven, Lewes, The Ouse Valley, Seaford, Eastbourne and Brighton". I had been given a copy, and it made me overly concerned about the threat of nuclear war.

Then, as part of our English lessons, we watched a programme called "Threads". It was a documentary style drama about a nuclear holocaust, its effect on the city of Sheffield, and the long term effects of nuclear war on civilization. It made me feel so sick that I had to ask to leave at one point. We also watched the film "When the Wind Blows" based on the book by Raymond Briggs. It featured the animated characters Jim and Hilda Bloggs during a nuclear attack. Having seen so much about the Falklands War when I was eleven years old, war, and especially nuclear war, was something that I believed was a real possibility. This affected me way more than I realised at the time.

Another film, released in 1987, that also had a deep impact on me, was "Cry Freedom". Set in the late 1970s, it was based on the real life events during the apartheid era of South Africa. It told the story of black activist Steve Biko who joined forces with white newspaper editor Donald Woods. Denzel Washington played Biko and Kevin Kline portrayed Woods. The film was a hard hitting look at discrimination, political corruption, and the repercussions of violence. I was fifteen, and I found it shocking that such injustice could even exist. The death of Steve Biko was a tragedy. I still find it hard to believe that when I was only four and a half years old, more than 700 school children were killed in the Soweto disturbances that began on 16th June 1976, and over 4000 were wounded by armed officials. Until I saw this film, I had not been particularly aware of apartheid or discrimination and I was really saddened. It made me pay much more attention to the news and the issues around apartheid. It certainly made me look at other cultures in a different way. Steve Biko stood up for what he believed in. Yes, he was an activist and even called a terrorist. In the same way that many peaceful animal rights activists here in the UK are still classed as terrorists, despite being peaceful. Just because someone stands up to authority for a just and moral cause does not make them a terrorist. Just because someone from another culture acts differently from us doesn't mean we should belittle them for it, or judge them for being different. Be it in belief, sexuality or skin colour, we live in a free world and freedom of expression is valued. Animals in the UK had better rights than black humans during apartheid. We don't necessarily have to agree with their belief or culture, but we do need to respect their culture as long as it is ethically and morally sound. This film really instilled into me a sense of justice and a need to be fair, not just to other people, but also to other living creatures.

I passionately believe that the suffering of any creature, be it human (of any race, creed, religion, gender), or animal including wildlife, domestic, agricultural, circus or zoo, is not to be tolerated. As well as other animal charities, these days I also support a number of human charities that deal with suffering.

Looking back, I realise that I was probably far more sensitive and upset by such things than most boys of my age. I was actually suffering from depression, though back then such a condition was not really recognised, especially in teenagers. A lack of confidence was called laziness.

But this depression affected my exam results and my ability to study. I found myself spending more and more time on my own, walking around in the countryside thinking about and struggling to recognise and deal with my emotions – as well as the usual struggles of a teenage lad. This was my escape from a world in which I really felt I needed to do something, but was unsure of quite what or how.

There were also a number of issues between my brother, my mum and me that I found very hard to cope with. My brother always did better than me at school, and when I got an "E" grade in my French studies in my yearly appraisal, it was a pretty humiliating experience. Being made, by my mum, to stand in front of the mirror and repeatedly say "Bon Jour" time and time again for what felt like hours, being shouted and screamed at because I couldn't pronounce it in a good enough French accent. This was a pretty low point in my relationship with my mum and made me feel even more of a failure, at a time when I was already struggling with my own self-confidence. But in retrospect, she was clearly doing what she thought was the right thing, and in my best interest. Although I might not have liked some of the decisions my parents made, or the way I was treated at times, I can now really appreciate the sacrifices they made for both me and my brother. It must be very hard being a parent.

But the upside of these emotionally tempestuous teenage times was that I felt the need to concentrate my mind on my conservation work, and would bury myself in various projects. The downside was that I would sometimes do this to the point of obsession. The result was that I tended to put people off and push them away from me. They would often laugh at me and claim that I was going through a mid-life crisis; that I was trying to take on and do so many different projects. Some even accused me of jumping on the latest band wagon and questioned my compassion and motives.

It seemed that the one thing I was really good at, had a natural instinct for and to which I was passionately committed – even that was being thrown back in my face.

Chapter 3 - Conservation In Action.

Although I started using my conservation work as an escape from the other pressures of life, it was also enjoyable, worthwhile and made me feel like I was actually achieving something, making a difference.

Whilst at school I had campaigned to get Hailsham's Common Pond cleaned up. Much to the annoyance of the Town Clerk and councillors, I would regularly attend the council meetings, asking questions and applying pressure over the dilapidated state of the pond.

The pond was man-made with a circular wall built out of old sewer bricks. Originally it was only about four to five feet deep, but years of neglect had led to the wall becoming very weathered. By the late 1980s the pond would virtually dry out every summer.

In a bungalow opposite the pond lived a lovely couple called Monica and Reg Gosden. I became good friends with Monica, "Mon" to her friends and also known as "The Duck Lady". I spent many hours with her, talking about the pond, watching the ducks and geese, and catching any which had problems. We also discussed its bad state of repair.

One weekend I decided to get people to write messages of support for the pond in a book, and why it should be cleaned up and maintained. I then presented this to the council in an attempt to get them to sort out the mess. With my conservation hat on I organised several Sunday tasks for volunteers clearing up the rubbish. The council paid for a skip, and we would get into the pond and spend the day splashing about in the water, pulling out shopping trolleys, milk crates, tin cans, bikes, old video recorders, scrap metal and much more.

But still the pond leaked, and the brick wall remained unrepaired. I had many an argument with the council over this, and eventually wrote a 7 page letter of complaint to the local paper. This resulted in an article being printed in the Hailsham Gazette on the 27th September 1989 entitled "Trevor Slams 'Pigsty' Town". In it I quoted from an environment report which stated "If local authorities allow a pigsty to develop, men will behave and act like pigs." I went on to describe the town as being "one large housing estate" and saying that the council were not doing enough to protect the town and its few remaining green spaces.

Not surprisingly neither the council nor my parents were very happy about this. The Town clerk accused me of stabbing them in the back with my vicious attack, but I also got letters of support in the paper, from people who agreed with my description of the town.

My young age meant I was prone to speaking my mind, and I certainly didn't know much about diplomacy at the time. But I still agree with my thoughts on the town and the state of it at the time. I am, however, pleased that although Hailsham has grown in size considerably over the years, green space has been built into developments, new parks created and Hailsham has still retained some of its market town character. I like to think that my youthful enthusiasm, if undiplomatic, did play some part in that.

One of my earliest rescues took place on Hailsham Common Pond. This involved, "Goo", the infamous goose. We always called "Goo" a she, but looking back, I suspect she was actually a he. She was always there right from the start, as far as I recall, and was very fond of Mon the duck lady. Mon would come out of her gate, call "Goo" at the top of her voice, and Goo and her two goose friends would come straight off the island and over to the side to get fed. We caught her a few times over the years when she had problems, and would take her to the vet's. In 1992 I had a frantic call from Mon. Goo was swimming round and round in circles and clearly in distress. We knew she was old and had poor vision in one eye, but the day came when she clearly had too many problems. With Mon's help we managed to catch Goo and, after a check-up at the local vets, it was found that she was blind and needed a new home and a family to look after her. Christine Powell who lived in Western Road, Hailsham, kindly took on Goo in her small garden park. Here she lived out the rest of her life. Goo even hit the front page of the Sussex Express when it was announced she was retiring.

In 1989, aged seventeen, I went to Sixth Form College, doing a course in Agriculture and Conservation.

Here I was encouraged to follow up various local environmental issues. One of these was at Summer Hill, just south of Hailsham, where a cement company had a filling yard. Whilst out on one of my many country walks, I came across its beautiful old brick-yard which had several ponds teaming with wildlife. Pond Skaters, Diving Beetles, Water Boatmen, Great Crested Newts, Dragonfly and Caddis Fly Larvae, frogs, toads, and so much more. There were 6ft high swathes of Rosebay Willow herb with its purple flower spikes. It was a great haven for wildlife. One afternoon I noticed a grey liquid on the footpath. I traced it back to find it was wet concrete being washed out of some cement mixers in the yard. The filling and washing station took up about a fifth of the old brick-yard. I started investigating further out into the site, away from the public footpath, and to my dismay I found a wall of concrete about 12ft high which was slowly engulfing this secret sanctuary of nature. Every day lorries would return from their rounds and wash out their tanks, dumping more and more concrete, which was slowly extending out to cover the plants and trees. It had even started pouring into one of the ponds.

I contacted a reporter at the Hailsham Gazette who came across to the site with me. He was not exactly dressed for the occasion in a white shirt, black trousers and posh black shoes. As we were walking along looking at the destruction, suddenly a wash of concrete from one of the lorries poured down the footpath covering his shoes. He was not happy, and agreed to contact both the council and the company who owned the site, and write an article. The back page of the following week's Gazette reported on the "Concrete Jungle pollution threat", with a picture of me standing at the base of the giant concrete wall of waste, with the remains of plants sticking out of its dried out top. The article even appeared on the front page of the Sussex Express on 10th August 1990. This resulted in members of East Sussex County Council visiting the site, and a spokesperson for the cement company denying there were any pollution problems.

This was one of the first environmental issues which I helped cover with my "Countryside Officer" hat on for 'Environment Hailsham' of which I was one of the founding members.

I also took on the role of Tree Warden for Hailsham. I would walk round some of the areas of building development to check on the condition of the trees, look for any developers in breach of the their planning agreements and then liaise with Wealden or the Town Council. It was during one of these trips that I noticed an unusual smell in the air. I then spotted a vapour coming out of the top of a tank from an industrial compound on Diplocks Industrial Estate. The tank had a chemical hazard symbol on the side, so I phoned Sussex Police to raise my concerns. The police duly arrived, and I told them that I would be working just up the road if they needed me.

About an hour later a police car turned up. A couple of policemen came and found me and asked me to accompany them back to the site. Apparently I needed to be checked over by paramedics. On arriving back at the industrial estate, I was amazed to find numerous fire engines, ambulances and police swarming all over the place. The road and area had been completely shut off and firemen in chemical hazard suits were coming out of the yard.

I was checked over in the ambulance and, due to a headache which had developed since breathing in the vapour, they decided to take me to Eastbourne District General Hospital for further assessment and tests. I was returned home later that day, but admitted again that evening suffering from breathing difficulties. I later found this was just a delayed panic attack from the shock of the incident. I suffered from headaches for about six weeks following this event, and I wrote to the company asking if they would make a donation to an environmental charity as a result of what I went through. Not surprisingly they refused to admit liability so I decided to seek legal advice. Eighteen months later, the company involved decided to settle out of court.

About this time I was going out with Alison, a girl from my sixth form. She introduced me to a piece of land I had not been to before. It was a common area for dog walkers at the old Groveland's Farm, what is now Gleneagles Drive, Hailsham. At the edge of the field next to the old St John Ambulance headquarters were the old farm buildings. There was a very long brick-built cow shed, and a brick barn with beautiful old oak beams. There were also a series of dove cotes and pigsties, laid out in a lovely pattern on either side of the main barn. There was a wooden stable area too. I was fascinated by the farm which had recently been sold to building developers, along with the farm land, and was now becoming sadly derelict.

The farm dated back to the thirteenth century. It was originally owned by a Robert de la Grave in about 1279 and had remained a farm until it was sold in 1988. Until then, for the previous seventy years, it had been in the Rumary family. Originally a dairy farm, it then changed to fat stock, corn and wheat. Brothers George and Stanley Rumary had taken over the farm from their father, and when Stanley married Betty they lived on the farm for 43 years.

By a curious coincidence, I was contacted by the granddaughter of Betty Rumary, the lady who owned the farm and who had sold it to the developers after her husband, Stanley died in 1987. She loved the buildings, and had asked the developers not to demolish them, but to put them to public use. Sadly the developers had other ideas. We contacted the Hailsham Gazette and its front page headline duly read, "Will Historical house make way for homes? Battle over Farm". Betty was quoted as saying, "When I sold the land last November, I asked for the barn and cow stalls to be saved because they are so lovely. I wouldn't like to see them come down but now that I've sold the land there's nothing I can do."

We tried to get the farm listed for its design, and the barn for being 13th century. The authorities, in their wisdom, said there were not enough characteristics in the buildings to list them.

Even though the listed status of the buildings failed, I was determined to see if there was another way that they might be saved from demolition. So, with Alison's help, I started a campaign. With the permission of the developers, we spent the summer months working with local volunteers, cleaning up the farmyard and clearing vegetation, trying to manage the site and keep it in good order. Sadly the old barn was targeted several times by thieves, who stole a large quantity of the old clay peg tiles from the roof, and by vandals who smashed up parts of the buildings.

The projected housing estate development inevitably took place. The main farm buildings still survive, and despite several attempts to turn them into community use, neither the local authority nor the developers had any desire to spend money on this. Most of the old apple trees in the orchard were felled. However, a communal garden has been created in the middle of the estate. This has become not just a peaceful oasis for human inhabitants, but also a small and precious haven for wildlife. I am proud to think that I played a small part in preserving at least this. It is now called Groveland's Orchard Park.

My girlfriend Alison had taken on a part-time job at Cophall Stables, where the Polegate Service Station is now. Despite having an allergy to horse dust I went with her every weekend to help out. I concentrated on the heavier outdoor jobs which Alison used to struggle with. I didn't get paid, but as a treat occasionally I would get the chance to have a ride out to the woods. Mind you I quite often had to wear goggles and a face mask, due to my allergy, which must have looked an odd sight.

We were asked by a relative of the stable's owner if Alison and I could help out directing the traffic at a car boot sale they were putting on. These eventually turned into what is now one of the biggest car boot sales in the area.

On the day of the boot sale, Alison wasn't feeling well so I went on my own. Half way through the day one of the stable-girls ran up to me in tears. She was in a dreadful panic because she had found one of the horses had caught its foot in some rusty metal in a hedge. I told her to run to the yard and get help and I dashed up to the field. When I arrived I found the horse standing there patiently. I gently stroked the horse's leg so it would get used to me to touching it, and then calmly lifted its foot. With some strength and force I managed to pull apart the metal, just enough to push it over the fetlock joint, and free the horse. I walked it slowly down the field towards the stables so it could be checked over and stabled for the night. The following week the horse's owner came to find me at the yard to thank me, and said anytime I wanted to ride, just ask. This was the first and last time I was involved with a horse rescue, but it wasn't the last time I was to have a close encounter with a horse; a rather high spirited Arab mare.

She belonged to the owner of the stables. I was walking her in from the fields to the stables which involved crossing some thick mud. In doing so the horse, which had a tendency to play up a bit, managed to step down hard on my foot. I let go of the horse and in complete agony, managed to get my foot out of the mud leaving my boot behind. The pain was horrendous and there was no way I could walk on my foot, so one of the stable-girls piled me into her wheelbarrow and trundled me back to the stable yard. I sat in the tack room shocked and in pain and had a good old-fashioned strong cup of tea with sugar – how very British! Eventually one of the adults came asked me if I was ok, I explained what had happened and they took me down to A&E at Eastbourne where my foot was x-rayed. I had been extremely lucky. My foot was not fractured but the bone was badly bruised and very swollen. There was no way I was going to get it back into my retrieved boot!

Despite this painful encounter, and the fact that I'm allergic to horses, I still really like them. I'm still allergic to them but it's not a severe as it used to be. I've since discovered I'm also allergic to deer!

Alison was having painful problems of a different order. She lived at home with her mother who was in the process of having a breakdown. At one point her mum had to be admitted to hospital. Alison was very upset and I was worried about how she would cope.

I asked my parents if she could come and stay with us, but Alison wanted to remain at her house as she had her dog and pet mice to look after. I spoke to my course tutor about it and he told me that I should spend some time with her. Apart from a few set classes, my hours at college were flexible, and I tried my best to go in and pick up work to do at her house. I also did my best to encourage her to come back to college. What surprised me more than anything was that no one noticed or seemed to care that she was living at home on her own. Alison had no money and no one, apart from me, to look after her. I stayed with her for two weeks, continuing to pop into college to see my English teacher and others, and trying to keep on top of my work. This was only possible because of the module-based course I was on. I knew my mum would neither have understood nor agreed to this, so I didn't tell her what I was doing.

Then one day my mum turned up at the door. She was outraged and extremely angry and marched me off home. Although I hated it at the time, I can see now how everyone just thought I was bunking off college. When I went back, my head of year pulled me out of class and also gave me a right telling off, saying how my previously good work had nose-dived, and I really had to buck my ideas up. I tried to explain why, but he just shouted at me telling me not to talk back, instead of allowing me to explain that I was trying to support someone who I cared about and who had a problem. Thankfully my English teacher was very supportive and eventually we managed to persuade Alison to return to college and finish her studies. I'm pleased to say we both passed.

As part of my college course I had to spend time working on a farm, something I really didn't want to do. I chose to go to Arlington Turkey Farm because of the conservation work that took place there. Generally their standards and their attitude towards the animals were good. Every Monday morning we had the job of plucking the freshly killed turkeys. Each time I plucked a feather I could smell an aroma of bacon. Not surprisingly I started hating bacon. By the end of my work placement I had become a proper vegetarian. I felt that if I couldn't bring myself to rear and look after an animal, nurture it, feed it, treat it, build it up, kill it, prepare it, cook it and then eat it, then I had no right to eat it in the first place. My father, who also worked at the farm at weekends, was and is able to do all that, and therefore I have absolutely no problem in him eating meat, but as far as some of my other friends and relatives are concerned they see meat as something that just comes off a shelf in a super market. An attitude I did not, and still do not, approve of.

I left college at the end of 6th form. I was hoping to go on to do a National Diploma course in Countryside Management and was even accepted for a place, but I couldn't raise the funds to go. I was also warned by the Downland Ranger that qualifications were not necessarily the best way of getting into a conservation job. He was just about to leave his council-paid job and there had been hundreds of applications for it. This worried me as I didn't want to leave college and be in debt and unable to find paid work. In the end I decided I would be better off continuing my voluntary work and developing my skills that way.

Alison and her mum had moved away from the area, to be closer to family in south east London just inside the Kent border. My parents had forbidden me to see her again as they said she was a bad influence on me. Not surprisingly, as a typical teenager, I ignored this demand. As a voluntary Local Groups Officer for the British Trust for Conservation Volunteers, I used to spend a lot of time running courses at weekends. Once a month I pretended I was off on a course, but instead would jump on the train to go and visit Alison.

After a while she got a live-in job at a kennels, which made it very difficult to contact her or see her. I tried phoning and even writing, but when I had not heard from her for almost six months, I stopped bothering. I was also having problems with my relationship with my mum. This was the start of her illness that the doctors were struggling to diagnose, and she was becoming increasingly worried.

All this was having a bad effect on my own health. I found myself continuing to feel isolated, alone and depressed, but also not understanding why and getting confused.

Ours was not exactly a close family, and emotions were felt to be a sign of weakness, so I found myself bottling up my feelings. The past five years had seen a number of issues which caused problems in the relationships between my mother, brother and I.

Most teenagers go through a rebellious stage and this seemed to stress my mum greatly. I tried my best to keep the peace so when my mum demanded that one of us do the washing up I would do it. On one occasion my mum told me, "If you turn out like your brother, I'll leave home."

I took this too literally. Having witnessed several parents of my class-mates divorce and how dramatic this was, it played heavily on my already delicate mental state. When I reached the teenage rebellious stage the relationship between my mum and I hit rock bottom, and for what felt like weeks at a time we would not talk to each other. After leaving college, and not hearing from my girlfriend, I started to experience feelings which I just couldn't understand and didn't know how to deal with. Looking back I feel sorry for my parents having to deal with all my teenage behaviour!

All this had been exacerbated by a potentially fatal car crash in 1989/90. My friend was driving when she was forced to swerve off the road by an overtaking vehicle coming at us head on round a bend. Our car mounted the grass verge, went up an embankment and was embedded in a hedge. Although neither of us was hurt, and the car was amazingly still driveable, we were both very shaken up. My friend in particular was extremely traumatized, and feeling I had to be strong for her, I suppressed my own shock and tried to comfort and reassure her as best I could.

But the accident had taken its toll. We could both have been killed and I found this reminder of my own mortality very disturbing. Visions of the incident haunted me for ages and caused me to lose a lot of sleep

In retrospect I am certain that all these swirling emotions that I was bottling up, keeping a good old stiff upper lip, led to my nervous breakdown. I sought help from Eastbourne Open Door Youth Counselling. The people there were wonderful and really helped me through this difficult time. I continued to go to counselling session for about eight months, and after a bit of encouragement found I was able to open up. For the first time I was able to talk about all the suppressed emotions and my mind gradually began to unscramble itself and I was gradually able to make sense of all that had happened. Thanks to the counsellors from Eastbourne Open Door, I began to develop a coping mechanism and my teenage anxieties and fears began to iron themselves out.

Looking back I can understand why my mother was so stressed. Parents are not taught how to look after children and teenagers. They had both been brought up by very strict parents, and that was all they had as a guide to rearing children. I can also see that my mum's frustration with her mysterious and undiagnosed illness was making the situation worse. Knowing my mum always felt a need to be in control, it must have been a very anxious time for her. She was also worried about keeping a roof over our heads and earning enough money to pay the mortgage, so when we ran up a huge phone bill and kept turning the heating up she wasn't best pleased. At one stage the doctors wouldn't believe she was even ill.

As a typical teenager I went through phases of being angry and frustrated with my parents; they were too strict, too controlling, intolerant and always worrying. Now I can see how very hard it was for them and how they coped with some very difficult situations as best they could, not least dealing with two problematic teenagers. My youthful frustration and anger has turned into adult appreciation and affection for two hard-working people who did their best for my brother and me. They made some huge sacrifices for us and helped support us in so many other ways - rather more than I observed many other parents doing for their offspring. As I'm not sure that I would do any better, it has rather discouraged me from having children of my own.

One job I really did enjoy, was working at Drusilla's Zoo Park during my summer holidays. It was to man the 'Rain Forest Story and Trading Post'. This was a small building in the zoo, where there was a rainforest exhibition; a greenhouse area landscaped with forest plants, a display of leaf cutter ants, humming birds, quail and a small pond. Attached to this was a shop selling Fair Trade goods. The centre was also used to raise awareness of the rainforest's plight and promoted "Programme for Belize". This was a charity launched in the UK in the late 1980s, initiated by the Massachusetts Audubon Society. They had set up "Programme for Belize" as a legal entity working closely with the Belizean Government and local people. The conservationist John A. Burton was appointed the UK representative and managed to get support from Sir David Bellamy and Sir David Attenborough along with many other eminent conservationists. The programme offered everyone a unique opportunity to save a magnificent tract of tropical rainforest containing a wealth of wildlife, helping to save five species of wild cat, over two hundred and fifty species of birds and many endangered plants. Around 70% of the migratory song birds found in North America spend the winter in Belize and adjacent parts of Central America.

At Drusilla's we offered people the chance to "purchase" and endow an acre of this rainforest. You would be given a certificate and information pack from "Programme for Belize" in return. We also had a forest wall. Children were offered the chance to attach a leaf to the wall in return for a donation of 25p or more towards saving the rainforest.

In the summer of 1990 I also led a sponsored walk along Eastbourne Seafront to raise money for "Programme for Belize". I wore a costume made out of plastic leaves and green trousers. We borrowed a stretcher from St John Ambulance and carried a wicker man along with us to help raise awareness.

I loved this work and found I was good at it. This not only helped to restore my confidence and recover from my breakdown, but it was also teaching me more about our endangered environment, the skills of fund-raising and charity work.

Chapter 4 - Chasing after birds - the feathered ones.

Although I still didn't have proper paid employment, I decided my best course of action was to continue with the voluntary conservation work I loved. I was learning all the time.

It was in the early 1990s, whilst doing some shrub clearance on the Downs, near Cow Gap, when I came across my first oiled Guillemots. We were clearing bushes close to the cliff edge, trying to protect the chalk grassland, and mowing to remove invasive grasses which smothered the shorter and rarer grassland plants.

One of the volunteers noticed two birds on the rocks at the bottom of the cliffs. We walked down the steps at Cow Gap whilst some of the volunteers stayed at the top looking down in order to guide us in. It was not an easy task to get there. The tide was well in and bashing against the rocks, making the chalk boulders very slippery. Dodging cold waves, we managed to make our way along to the birds which were covered in thick black oil. Soaking wet, we returned to the others, where Downland Ranger, Alan, wrapped them in newspaper and then drove me and the birds to Seaford. To the home of a wonderful lady who ran a small bird hospital.

Meta Mann was an inspiration to me. Her dedication and commitment to these oil-sodden birds was truly amazing, and I found myself with an overwhelming urge to help her and the casualties she took in.

Every winter I would jump on the bus at Hailsham and head for Polegate. Here I would either get on the train to Eastbourne, Seaford, Newhaven or Brighton, and then walk along the coast checking for oiled birds. Armed with a towel and a carrier, when I found one, I would take the bus to Seaford and walk to Meta's house for her to treat it.

I helped her clean out the cages and wash the birds. Every winter people like Meta, and organisations like the RSPCA, would deal with hundreds of oiled birds from the beaches of East Sussex alone. The oil was mainly from tankers washing out their dirty tanks before filing up again in ports. We also found a lot of evidence of oil being stored in inappropriate containers, like drinks' bottles from smaller boats that had been washed over the side.

Once the birds were strong enough, Meta would wash them in her bath and then treat them with Pepto-Bismol. This helped with any digested oil. When the birds were fit and healthy enough, they were collected by the RSPCA and driven down to their main wildlife hospital, West Hatch, in Somerset. I spoke several times to a man called Colin Seddon, and received a letter from him complimenting Meta's work. He said that of all the birds that were sent to him, what a good condition hers were in, and that she had one of the best success rates with the oiled birds.

Thankfully, it is now illegal for ships to wash out their tanks whilst at sea. They now have to pay to clean out their tanks in port before refilling. Finding oiled birds doesn't happen quite as often as it used to.

In March 1990 whilst undertaking more Downland Management with the council's ranger, we had a visit from the then Member of Parliament for Eastbourne, Ian Gow. He came to see our work, and spoke to most of the volunteers. He seemed genuinely interested in what we were doing, and the fact that we did it on a voluntary basis. In a letter to me after his visit, he said he was very impressed with our approach to dealing with local problems; "Unlike other people who would say, 'that's not my problem', and let someone else sort it out, you say, 'there is a problem and what can I do to help'. I came away greatly encouraged by your commitment to improve our environment, and by your recognition that we are trustees of a marvellous heritage, which we have a duty to pass on, uninjured, to those who will come after us."

These words really encouraged me to do even more to help, as I could see that if we all took the "It's not my problem" attitude, society and our environment would end up being in even more of mess.

In 1991 Meta phoned me and asked if I would go to Deanland Caravan Park at Golden Cross to check out a report of some ducks covered in oil. I jumped on the next available bus and walked the mile journey to the park. There I found a small pond near "Fox Hollow". The fumes were horrendous. The whole pond was covered with a shiny film. This turned out to be heating oil. There were about 30 ducks and moorhens on the pond many of which were smothered in oil. I spoke to the park's management and told them I had no choice but to contact the National Rivers Authority, or NRA, (now known as the Environment Agency). While I was there a guy came into the office and asked if he could order some more heating oil as squirrels had damaged a pipe coming out of his tank. We asked him when this had happened, and he said it had been a couple of days ago.

The NRA sent an officer out who started working with the site owners on the clean-up operation. I phoned Meta, and we set about catching the ducks.

The RSPCA then arrived, looked at the situation and wished us luck in catching them. They said it would be virtually impossible to do so, and then they left. Although I didn't appreciate it at the time, I am now well aware of how busy they are, and how they lack the resources to spend hours on end at incidents like this.

As a volunteer I had plenty of time to sort out a rescue mission and virtually lived on site for a week. Out of thirty or so ducks, we caught at least twenty two. Many of them were hiding in the box hedges. Having blocked off the exits, I would then crawl in and catch then. A number of residents also asked us if we could catch those ducks that had hidden under their caravans.

This rescue mission resulted in my first broadcast interviews, with BBC Southern Counties Radio and TVS, the regional TV company. I inadvertently managed to land myself in a bit of hot water. One of the clean-up workers had told me that the absorbent material they were using to clear the oil was going to be dumped in nearby woodland. I mentioned this on the live radio interview, and to the NRA. As a result, I found that the following morning the clean-up workers had been instructed not to speak to me.

I also started volunteering with the Sussex Amphibian and Reptile Group, who monitored the local Toad Migration routes. Some of the staff at Drusilla's asked me if I would be interested in helping out with patrols at the migration site along the Cuckmere Valley. Not having my own transport was a problem; however various people used to give me a lift across there and I would help with the patrols. Using a van we would drive along slowly, two of us sitting with our legs dangling out of the back, and every time we came across a toad we would jump off, pick it up and place it in a bucket. Then we would take our toad collection down to the nearest dyke and release them.

During February, March and April, depending on the weather conditions, the toads would migrate from Friston Forest across the Litlington village to Exceat road and onto the flood plains of the Cuckmere Valley. One year a count took place and over 10,000 toads had been moved in one season by a huge army of volunteers. Scores of people, with torches, buckets, wellington boots and gloves, would patrol the area gathering up toads and moving them to safety. The unfortunate thing was, the toads preferred to move at night, when there is light rain and mild temperatures. Pleasant for the toads, but not quite so pleasant for us! Neither was the male toads' defence mechanism, to pee on you. Hence the reason for wearing gloves.

For those who don't know much about toads, the males are the small ones and the females are the large ones. Now, the males are not daft. They would sit on the warm damp surface of the roads waiting for a female to come along, then climb onto her back and hold on round her neck. The female, desperate to get to the water to spawn, would then have to carry the male down to the water too. It was not uncommon to see two or three males hanging on for dear life, hitching a lift down to the water.

I was made aware of a building development off Arlington Road East, in Hailsham. There were concerns over a pond that had Great Crested Newts living in it and was going to be filled in. I remember finding these newts as a child and decided to go and investigate. Unfortunately the pond had already been bulldozed, but to our surprise we found numerous newts in a large water-filled trench about 35ft away. It was a Friday evening and there was no one I could contact. So I placed a notice on the developer's office door and left an answerphone message with English Nature, now Natural England, and part of the Department of Environment, Food and Rural Affairs - DEFRA.

Working with some friends, Anne and Lorraine, we spent the weekend netting the newts and moving them to new sites where Great Crested Newts were known to be, including a pond at Bates Green Farm, Arlington.

On Monday the developers were not very happy with us. I apologised and reminded them that I don't write the law, I just follow it. Wealden District Council and English Nature then got involved. It was agreed that our actions were acceptable, but only as an emergency measure, and a licence had to be retrospectively applied for, with an action plan to return the newts to the area.

I was in my late teens, and being expected to apply for a licence and write an action plan was pretty daunting. It took me months; and all the while a "Stop" order had been placed on the development in that part of the site. The building company were so annoyed with me they threatened to sue me for the interruption and costs. I reminded them that I was not getting paid for this, and they were welcome to employ a professional conservationist who could do it more quickly - and more expensively. Amazingly, that was the last I heard from the developers. A couple of years later the building work was finally completed. With the help of Barry Kemp, from the Sussex Amphibian and Reptile Group, we fulfilled the conditions of the licence by moving a number of baby newts back to the area.

My wildlife education continued to expand when I met Janet. She was a very knowledgeable lady and introduced me to the County Council's Wild Flower Verge Scheme. This was a new project that looked at changing the management of grass verges at locations where there were rare plants or a diverse plant life. I helped Janet visit some of the sites and record the plants, drawing up lists of the species present. She was a terrific teacher and taught me a great deal. She showed me a number of amazing plants that otherwise I wouldn't have known even existed. I was fascinated by the local orchid population, especially the early purple orchids, the green winged orchids and the pyramidal orchids. But the most amazing specimen I found was the Bee Orchid, on a downland path near Polegate. Getting up close and seeing them in such detail was wonderful.

I would often go for walks at night, and one evening coming back from Upper Dicker along the edge of the A22 Hailsham By-pass, I came across a badger that had been hit by a car, but was still alive. I had no idea what to do so ran the short distance home and called the RSPCA. They were not available. Not knowing what else to do, I took a large pet carrier back to the badger and carefully picked him up and placed him inside. But sadly, within minutes it died. I was devastated. I later found out that the badger's spine was broken, and moving it probably sped up its death. I was determined to find out how I might be able to help such animals. It was clear that there just weren't enough people willing and able to assist with such emergencies.

I was soon introduced to the Southdowns' Badger Group and a man called Des. I learnt a lot from him, as well as other members of the group, and became involved in badger sett surveys, checking badgers, and investigating possible illegal activity.

In the early 1990s, The Ministry of Agriculture had undertaken a study which involved sending dead badgers for post mortem examinations and BTb testing. Working with the badger group, I would go out and pick up these animals. The smell was horrendous at times, and we would have to drive along with the windows open. On one occasion the stench was so bad that I threw up out of the window. But it was a small price to pay if we could help establish how many badgers carry bTB and the degree of risk the badgers posed to cattle.

That was over twenty years ago, and this question still hasn't been satisfactorily answered, or the problem solved.

I was also asked to survey a number of sites in East Sussex for possible badger digging. In the five years I spent checking setts I found five which had been disturbed but only one, near Newhaven, which showed evidence of having been successfully dug out. Several years later we found another at Hellingly. I don't know how true this was, but I was told that a live badger for illegal baiting would be sold for up to £2,000.

I spent a lot of time undertaking sett survey work and monitoring the local badger population. I would walk from my parents' home in Hailsham along public footpaths, through woodlands and fields, checking for badger setts and any interference and eventually arriving at a friend's home at East Hoathly where I would often stay. This was close to where a badger sett had been tampered with, and we kept a regular check on the area looking for evidence of illegal interference. Several times I joined forces with the local

Dog Warden, and members of the local badger group to check setts further afield.

I was contacted by a couple of people who started passing me information about the activities of a group that were suspected of being involved in illegal wildlife crime. The information was always vague, and always after the event, which was very frustrating. I passed the information on to an appointed person within the Badger Group who was overseeing my work. I built up a list of vehicle numbers, names and details of people who may have been involved in these apparent crimes, and I would forward all this to the Badger Group. I understood that this was then being passed on to one of Sussex Police's Wildlife Liaison Officers based at Brighton.

Some of the reports I received were about poached deer that had been caught and killed with crossbows, and being hung and butchered in garages; birds of prey being shot, and foxes being dug out of dens and terriers set on them, ripping them apart. I found some of what I was being told deeply sickening, but felt reassured that the information I was gleaning might eventually lead to a prosecution. The issue that concerned me the most though, was the digging of badger setts to catch live badgers.

Somehow, word had got out that I was watching and monitoring these activities. I informed the person supervising me, explained the situation and was advised not to tell the police. I decided to go against this advice. The following day I found a couple of local police inspectors knocking on my door. They were suspicious about what I was doing. I apologised to them, and asked them to contact the Wildlife Liaison Officer at Brighton for more details, and then come back to me. A day later, two officers from Special Branch turned up wanting to speak to me. By then I had managed to speak to the Wildlife Liaison officers at Brighton, and had agreed to give them all the information I had collected. It soon became clear that a lot of the details I had been passing to my contact in the Badger Group had not been passed on to the Police. Quite rightly they had concerns about what I was up to and whether I was an animal rights activist – a terrorist. It was clear that my contact within the Badger Group had been acting independently of the group when he decided not to share all the information with the police.

I received several threats as a result of my work and a dead fox was dumped on our home doorstep. The police also warned me to stay away from various pubs and areas that they deemed unsafe for me to be seen at. I just hadn't realised quite what a risk I had been taking investigating illegal badger activity, nor what danger I had been putting my family in. This was an eye opener for me, and I decided to take a back seat with this type of animal welfare work.

But I was becoming more and more frustrated at not having my own transport and, despite passing my driving test in January 1990, it would be a few more years before I could afford a car. In order to buy a car, I needed money, and in order to earn money, I needed a job.

Chapter 5 - Old and Modern Technology.

One of my first full time jobs was working as a trainee tree surgeon. It was a good experience and one I really enjoyed, but perhaps it wasn't the best sort of work for someone who was rather accident prone, and I only did it for about six months.

There were two incidents which made me realise I might not be best suited for working with chain saws and dangling from trees. We had a contract to undertake some woodland management up in East Horsley in Surrey. I was asked to go across to an island to do some work on a Crack Willow Tree, the wood that they make cricket bats out of. I had been trained in using ropes and harness and with these slung over my shoulder I waded across the pond and organised my ropes. With Crack Willow you have to be careful, as it is hard and will snap under pressure, and I was warned I needed to have a decent undercut whilst cutting back limbs. I threw my rope up over the highest branch I could reach, attached my harness and started my climb. I had to change my anchor point several times but eventually I was about 30ft off the ground, in the heart of the tree with a good view cross the entire lake and grounds. I pulled up my chain saw, pulled on the starter cord and the engine roared into life. With my hard hat, visor, and ear protection in place I started to cut back branches, removing crossing branches and generally tidying up.

There wasn't too much work to be done of this tree and I had left the hardest bit till last. It was by far the largest part I had to remove. I did my undercut and then started my top cut. Suddenly there was an almighty crack which made me drop the chainsaw. I felt as though I was being thrown back and forth against the tree trunk, like a bat with an elastic ball attached.

I sat there immobilised with shock, hugging the trunk of the tree. It was about five minutes before I could move. The safety catch on the chainsaw had been tripped so that wasn't a worry, but I absolutely ached all over. Pulling myself together I managed to restart my chainsaw and tidy up my cut then lowering myself down to ground level. I felt numb all over and had to take a break before wading back to the bank. I've never felt anything like that before, or thankfully, since. I must have been concussed as a result of the incident and had to take a couple of days off.

The other incident, which still makes me laugh when I think about it, was at Rotherfield, working at a large mansion house. At the back of the house was a tiered garden. Between each tier was a stone wall about 12-15ft high, with flower borders in front of it. We were working at the very top level on a group of mature beech trees that needed routine maintenance. My boss Roger climbed the trees and chopped the branches, while I was at their base clearing the ground as my boss dropped down the branches. All of a sudden I found myself falling and spinning round. Accidentally I had stepped back and fallen from the top tier. Luckily I was wearing a safety helmet, which cracked when I hit the wall of the second tier, and then I bounced down to the very bottom of the garden. I briefly passed out, and came round to the sound of laughter. Virtually all the workmen undertaking a refit of the house had seen me fall, and they were all in stitches, including my boss up the tree. It was, apparently, like a scene from a cartoon. I was very lucky that I didn't do anything more than injure my wrist which had to be X-rayed at the hospital. It still makes me laugh thinking about it, though there could have been a much more serious outcome, and it made me reconsider my career as a tree surgeon. Did I mention I was accident prone?

While undertaking badger sett surveys around the village of East Hoathly, I often stayed with a lady who lived in the village. She introduced me to my first long term job at Abacus Research, a market research company based in Uckfield. I started working part time in their phone room, calling people and asking questions and then filling out paper questionnaires. Computers were not commonplace in those days. It was a boring and monotonous job, but it gave me an income and the hours were flexible too. I soon realised that surveys are not all they are cracked up to be. If you ask the right questions in the right way, you can get any answer you want.

In the summer of 1993 I was asked to undertake a sett survey at Groombridge on the disused railway line, now the Spa Valley Railway. A team working on the line was concerned about the presence of a badger sett and the legalities of the work they were undertaking. I paid them a visit and was able to advise them. As a result I was asked to write a management

46

plan for the section of track they were working on. I spent many hours on this line and walked its entire length from Groombridge to Tunbridge Wells. It passes through some stunning Sussex countryside and is well worth a visit.

Throughout my late teenage years I would try and stay with friends as often as I could. Anyone who has had to deal with typical Harry Enfield "Kevin and Perry" type teenagers will know what my brother and I were like; spending hours on the phone speaking to friends, turning the heating up in the evening whilst only wearing T-shirts, eating everything in sight, not washing up, expecting someone else to do our washing etc. We certainly had our moments!

Inevitably, this led to many an argument with our mother. She was a workaholic and constantly worried about how bills were going to be paid and how she could save up for one thing or another.

She had also started having problems with her health, but as she didn't make a fuss about it, in true teenage fashion we didn't realise how much of a problem this was causing her. But then neither did she, nor the doctors. For several years she battled with them, and was sent for one test after another to try and find out why she was having difficulty digesting food properly. The longer the problems went on the more frustrated she became. At times this really seemed to upset her and as a result she wasn't always nice to be around.

Eventually she was diagnosed as having Coeliac Disease, and once she finally knew what was wrong, she seemed to calm down a lot. This coincided with both my brother and I spending less time at home, which really helped our relationship. Slowly we began to be able to build bridges. For several years she managed to control her disease, double checking everything she ate to ensure it didn't contain wheat gluten. It made cooking and eating out difficult. These days it's not uncommon to see gluten free food on menus, but back in the 1990s it was unheard of, and the quality and taste of food without gluten was pretty poor too. I remember trying to cook gluten free cakes in the microwave. They came out like pancakes and tasted of not very much.

During the summer of 1993 my mum's illness became worse. She lost weight and had to take time off work. Because I saw her on an almost daily basis, I didn't really notice the slow changes in her. But my brother was away, training as a nurse at Pembury Hospital, and when he came home one weekend he took one look at her and called out the doctor. Later that day she was admitted to hospital. I still feel guilty for not noticing her decline. Because our family didn't talk openly about feelings and emotions, I found it very difficult to talk to my mum, or to know what to say or do. She was diagnosed as having a bowel infection, and was confined to a side room for about six weeks while on treatment. Examinations revealed bowel polyps, and several of them had to be surgically removed.

No one really sat me down and talked to me about what was going on, or what anything meant, and I struggled to take in what was happening and how seriously ill my mum was. She did improve however, and was eventually moved onto the main ward. My mum hated sitting still. She was up and about, but still on treatment, and had to stay in hospital as she was struggling with her diet and to keep her weight up. At the worst point she weighed just under five stone.

She was in Eastbourne District General Hospital and there were real problems with their catering department getting my mum's diet right. It got so bad that she stopped ordering food from them. I would cycle down every midday with her lunch, and my father would visit after work in the evening and take her dinner. Not having transport, I still had to cycle everywhere, or catch the bus.

I became really frustrated with the hospital management and catering staff. Nurses on the ward encouraged me to write a letter of complaint. So I wrote to my local MP, my doctor, the Chief Executive of the Hospital, the head of the department, head of catering, the local NHS board and various other local contacts. In total, I must have sent out about twenty letters of complaint. A few days later, I arrived at the hospital to find my mum surrounded by numerous hospital managers. She was a bit upset and rather overwhelmed by the attention. I wasn't at all happy with them as they had not done me the courtesy of contacting me before speaking to her.

A few months later, in October 1993, I was at work when I received a call from the hospital. They told me that they were trying to get hold of my father and wanted him to come down to the hospital. I went straight home where my father had just arrived back from work. We headed down to the hospital and met the doctor. It was only then that I realised how seriously ill my mother was.

The 'Cancer' word had not been used by anyone and I had no idea that was what she had, until now. The news left me stunned and unable to take in what I was being told. I went to find the doctor, and asked him if we could sit down and have a chat. He explained the situation in a more down to earth way that I could then understand. I was able to ask him questions which allowed me to fully appreciate what was going on. The short version was that she had cancer and, despite treatment, the growth had increased and was now considered terminal. The doctors told us that mum could live a fairly normal life for about six months or more, but at some point she was likely to go downhill rapidly.

My mum, bless her, always tried to keep a stiff upper lip and I was really pleased that she was up and about and carrying on as normally as she could. Even at the end of November she was laughing and joking helping to put up the Christmas decorations around the ward. During my lunch-time visits, I would pick up one of the women's magazines from the shop at the entrance of the hospital, and we would read the funny stories from parents about their children, and the hilarious things they would say or do. We often had the whole ward in fits of laughter.

She clearly didn't like being stuck in hospital and we asked the doctor's permission to in bring Sam, our dog. So as not to be seen by too many people, we were let in via the fire escape and taken up to the ward. Sam was delighted to see her again, wagging her tail and a real fuss was made of her. She was such a lovely dog.

One weekend I was away working on the management plan for the Spa Valley Railway. When I got home I found most of my relatives there. My mum had taken a turn for the worse and had started to decline rapidly. I was annoyed and upset that no one had tried to contact me. In order to give my father some private time with her I didn't go to visit mum till the next day.

The following morning I went to the hospital on my own to see her. I struggled to cope with her condition. She was a completely different person from the one I had visited just three days ago. She was pale, weak, and very tired. It was a huge shock. I didn't know what to do or what to say. We sat in silence for ages. She passed away later that day. I was devastated. The relationship between my mum and I had greatly improved that year, but there were things still unsaid and I wish we had been given more time.

I had always felt I was a disappointment to my parents, so it meant a lot to me when one of the patients on the ward told me how proud mum was of me and the voluntary work I was doing. Even now this is one of my biggest driving forces, hoping that she is proud of me and what I have achieved.

That Christmas was very hard and with my birthday in January it was even more difficult. Christmas and Birthdays have not been the same without her ever since, and even now I prefer not to make a big deal out of them. I still miss her.

I was worried that my mum's death might lead me once again to start bottling up my deep felt emotions so I decided to go back to Open Door. I was sent to see a counsellor in Bexhill who really pushed me to examine how I was feeling, and more importantly, helped me to identify what I was feeling and why. She certainly assisted me in weathering that emotional storm, and I think had it not been for her counselling I would be a lot more intolerant of other people and their problems. But unfortunately this has also led me, on occasions, to being more susceptible to sympathising with some people who have then taken advantage of me as a result. That in turn has made me wary of misplaced compassion. It's all a bit of a double-edged sword!

After my mum's death I isolated myself, burying myself in my paid and voluntary work. Abacus decided to go digital and bring in computers, and I was one of the people they asked to help with the programming. I quickly excelled at this, and after a few years was promoted to Telephone Centre Manager. This involved computer programming, managing the digital side of the surveys and the staff. I worked very long hours, starting early and finishing late. If anything went wrong with the programming I was called in to fix it and to problem solve. It was not uncommon for me to work through the night in order to meet deadlines and produce results for the management and directors by first thing in the morning. It was getting very stressful with so much work being put on my shoulders, and one day I hung a sign on my back saying "I'm not God. I can't perform miracles!" This caused great amusement among my colleagues and the management, but they soon got the message that I needed some additional help.

I met some lovely people while I was working there. One person in particular stands out, Rosemary. She was everyone's granny in the phone room, worrying about us and taking care of us. She enjoyed a laugh but at the same didn't stand for any nonsense, which I liked.

When I became a manager, my life became a little easier as the company agreed to give me an interest-free loan with which I could buy my first car and get on the road. At last I was able to get to and from work under my own steam. It also enabled me to be even more flexible and independent, especially when it came to my wildlife rescue and conservation work. This marked a big step forward in my life.

Chapter 6 - Finding my feet.

Once I had wheels my ability to deal with rescue requests rapidly increased. But so did their frequency – most days I would get at least one call for help. This was partly because some of the others involved with wildlife rescue in the area had, for one reason or another, ceased to operate.

When I first started rescuing animals there were various individuals who, like me, were based at their homes, rescuing wildlife when not at work. There were ten in all; two in Hastings, one in Bexhill, two in Eastbourne, one in Seaford, one in Peacehaven, two in Brighton and one in Lancing.

In addition there were five charities with facilities for wildlife that took in animals; the Raystede Centre at Ringmer, the Kit Wilson Trust at Hadlow Down, the RSPCA Mallydams Wood Centre at Hastings and Folly Wildlife Rescue which was based just north of Crowborough.   There was also Redbrook Wildlife Rescue at Buxted which existed for a number of years, and then had to close down.

Most of those who did rescues from their homes, fitting it in between work, were forced to close down over time. The demands were, and still are, enormous and at times extremely stressful. There's the constant expectation from the public that you should be there when they demand it, regardless of whether you've not slept for 24 hours, or that you have a job to hold down to pay the bills in order to rescue the casualties. Home phones would ring at all hours of the day or night or people with injured animals would just turn up on your doorstep. All this making it very difficult to have any form of quality of life, and family and health problems were the most common reasons for people having to close down.

The more individuals closed down, the more calls I began to receive, and the more rescues I undertook. I decided the time had come to think of a name for my one-man operation. "East Sussex Wildlife Rescue" was the name I chose.

But I found myself in a difficult situation.

Although I could rescue the casualties, and give them basic treatment or take them to the vets, there just weren't enough people who could take in and tend the animals during their recovery period. It was also quite frustrating that the veterinary centres were not very enthusiastic in helping either. They were more than happy to euthanize casualties but not at all keen on treating them. And veterinary costs are not cheap. I was paying about £25 per X-ray and often antibiotics would cost between £4 and £12 per casualty on top of the consultation fee which was about £30 a time. While they will euthanize a wild animal for free, when it came to x-rays or medication, I had to pay for the treatment.

I did however find a very good vet, Robin Hooper, from Downwood Vets at Horam. Robin was very sympathetic, but also realistic about what we could achieve. He was very easy to talk to, he listened and explained what he was doing, and why we could or could not do something. I found it especially useful to hear him go through the pros and cons of a situation, and that he allowed me to go behind the scenes to watch procedures. Out of hours I would occasionally provide an additional pair of hands. I learnt a lot from Robin and, unlike many of the other vets I would call out of hours, he never once raised his voice or spoke to me as though he thought I was wasting his time on wildlife instead of domestic pets or farm animals.

Once the casualties had been given first aid and treatment, I would then take them to one of the local organisations like Folly Wildlife Rescue, Redbrook Wildlife Rescue, RSPCA Mallydams, Kit Wilson Trust, Rogers Wildlife Rescue, Raystede, Fox Project, Sussex Bat Hospital, Swan Sanctuary or Badger Group. All of these were very dedicated, supportive and helpful.

No one getting started in this line of work does so without making mistakes. I for one certainly did. One of the first hedgehogs I dealt with was covered in fleas so I sprayed it. Within hours it was writhing in agony and fitting. I later discovered that the particular flea spray I'd applied causes paralysis in hedgehogs. Sadly the hedgehog did not survive. I was very disturbed by this and began looking into the care and treatment of wildlife in much more detail.

I joined the British Hedgehog Preservation Society, the British Wildlife Rehabilitation Council and attended symposiums given by the Fox Project and BWRC at the Zoological Society of London. I tried to spend as much time as possible working and learning from as many organisations as I could.

Although I had stepped down as the warden for Hailsham Common Pond, I remained involved with it during 1993 and 1994. Several times I had to rescue domestic ducks that had been dumped on it. Although some were healthy, many were in poor condition and clearly would have suffered had they been left. I managed to get an article published in the local paper that asked people not to abandon unwanted ducks there.

I was also working with Lancing Wildlife Rescue. They had been asked by the Swan Sanctuary to rescue a family of swans at a new lake near Gleneagles Drive, Hailsham. One of the cygnets had a bad leg infection. The Swan Sanctuary thought it best that they should be taken in as a family. Once again I found myself getting into hot water. I had been working with several people who were standing as local town councillors, and although I had absolutely no need to inform them of what I was doing with rescues, they felt they were being left out of the loop, so when local residents asked what had happened to "their" swans, they didn't know and couldn't answer any questions. People get very over protective about the so call "special" species like swans, deer, seals and so on, and can become very defensive about what happens to them. As a result I ended up being accused by some councillors of catching various birds unnecessarily and taking them to rescue centres. It was even debated at a council meeting whether I should be banned from all Hailsham Town Council property, although the first I heard of this was when I was contacted by the person who had been listening to the debate at this public meeting, who was concerned that I had not been present to represent myself at the meeting.

This animosity was beginning to get out of hand. Whilst trying to help a person who'd been involved in a car accident, a council employee pitched up and began telling everyone, at the top of his voice, "Be careful or he'll disappear you to Hospital and you'll never be seen again". I was horrified, embarrassed, angry and upset by this and ended up walking away.

Fortunately I had the backing of the more experienced rescue organisations, and, having consulted a solicitor, I threatened the council with legal action.

Once I had provided the council with the veterinary notes from the Swan Sanctuary explaining why we had taken the birds, they backed off and the subject was never raised again. Sadly it put me off attending rescues on council property, and I would only go if the council contacted me and asked for my help. I found this negativity towards my rescue work quite hard to deal with, especially as it was coming from people I had originally thought of as friends who seemed to change drastically when they turned into local councillors.

What with events like that, and the death of my mum, I was becoming quite depressed. It was as though the one thing which gave me confidence and strength was being questioned. Once again I began to isolate myself more and more and buried myself in my paid job, rescue and conservation work the best I could.

In 1990, a film was released which was to have rather disastrous results for those animals in the class chelonia, (which comes from the Greek word 'kelone', meaning interlocking shields or armor), terrapins and turtles. While "Teenage Mutant Ninja Turtles" was to become one of the most popular and highest grossing films of all times, the real creatures upon which they were based became sad victims of its success.

Although terrapins had been kept as pets, and many subsequently abandoned long before the film was released, there was no doubt that its huge popularity increased the numbers of people buying them.

Over the next few years, I received numerous calls from people about dumped terrapins. I contacted a number of organisations but apart from Raystede, who were taking in quite a few, no one else was dealing with them. Thousands across the country were being sold as small baby terrapins. People would buy them without realising how big they would become.

Those who were trying to breed them to make a fast buck fortunately usually failed in their attempt as terrapins need quite a specialist environment.

It was a different story for those who thought they'd make charming little pets. The terrapins would out-grow their surroundings and people would give them up for the next new craze. Terrapins and turtles can also be very aggressive. They are carnivores and will eat more or less anything that moves, including snapping at children's fingers or duck's legs. More and more frequently we started getting calls about dumped terrapins and also had reports of them catching and pulling ducklings under the water and drowning them.

Realising the extent of this problem, in the mid-nineties I set up the National Terrapin Project and started collating data on the number of terrapins dumped across the country. Following an article in the BBC Wildlife Magazine, I received reports of over 222 ponds and lakes across the UK estimated to contain up to 2,000 terrapins. One of the biggest collections of terrapins was at Roath Park Lake in Cardiff where almost 100 terrapins had been dumped.

The project helped raise awareness of the effects of dumping terrapins in the wild and, working with the University of Wales, we highlighted their plight. It was thought that every year hundreds of terrapins were abandoned and, unable to hibernate properly, dying every winter. After working on the project for a couple of years, I hope I made a difference. I wish I had been older and more knowledgeable to have pushed further forward with it, but being in my early 20s I decided my best course of action was to pass over all the information I had collated for others to take up the reins.

Over the next few years I remained fairly quiet, working in the background, responding to calls and doing my best for the animals I came across. Then one day in 1996, I had rather literally, something of a sea-change in my rescuing career.

Whilst at work one morning, I received a phone call from Gary at Redbrook Wildlife Rescue. He asked me if I had any experience of dealing with oiled seabirds. Well of course I had. He told me that The Sea Empress tanker had hit rocks and was leaking oil at Milford Haven. Without a moment's thought I was on my way home to pack my bags and heading for Gary's house.

We loaded his ambulance with cages and medications and met up with Alan Knight, who was later to play a significant role in my life, Mark, Lis and other members of British Divers Marine Life Rescue. Off we drove in convoy with two Rigid Inflatable Boats in tow.

By nightfall we were in Wales, driving down dark narrow roads and finally arriving at Dale Fort Field Centre at St Anne's Head, near where the Sea Empress had hit rocks. Gary and I set up a temporary treatment centre in one of their classrooms. Members of Greenpeace and British Divers Marine Life Rescue would go out searching the coast line for oiled seabirds, and then bring them back to us for treatment.   We set up a reception area, where the birds would be assessed and treated, a holding area, a recuperation area and an area for birds that were being washed.   The system worked well. The cleaned, washed and stable birds were

transported down to the RSPCA centre at West Hatch, some to St. Tiggywinkles and some to the Swan Sanctuary. Only the birds that were fit enough to be transported would be moved. As a result the majority of our birds survived.

This was more than could be said about the fate of birds being dealt with by other organisations. Some were transporting oil-covered birds to the RSPCA without them being washed, cleaned or stabilised first. It was a long journey involving hours in the back of a van. The biggest problem with moving oiled birds is the fumes. If you have a lot of birds in the back of a vehicle breathing in oil fumes, they will develop lung damage.

What frustrated me more than anything was the way the local authorities did not seem to be able to make any decisions. For the first week the weather conditions were favourable and kept the oil contained in the harbour.   There were also nesting seabirds on the cliffs between Milford Haven and Tenby, so rescue teams had to keep clear of those areas to avoid frightening birds into the water. A week into the disaster, the authorities did not appear to have made any concrete decisions on how to move forward. Not surprisingly, the weather changed the following week and the oil started spreading out of the harbour and along the coast.

We had visited Tenby in the first week of our stay. It had a golden sandy beach, a picturesque harbour and an island just off shore. It was stunningly beautiful. The following week it was covered in oil that stuck to everything. The entire length of the beach and the harbour was black and shiny and stinking of fumes. The largest number of birds in one delivery came from here.

We went out on the boats a couple of times to help with the rescues. The sights were horrific. The number of dead birds floating around in the oil was just too many to count, and the effort that the BDMLR put into catching and rescuing the live birds was amazing. Using dry suits and ropes, and by guiding their boats in carefully, their volunteers were able to climb onto the slippery rocks to catch those birds that had managed to climb out of the water to some form of safety. I take my hat off to all of them, and the lengths to which they went to rescue those birds.

Gary and I stayed at Milford Haven for about two weeks and in that time over 300 birds were dealt with. Sadly many of them died, especially those that were severely oiled. It was horrendous, and still remains the worst two weeks of my life for feeling so helpless and hopeless amidst such scenes of devastation.

Having used up almost all of my paid holiday, I was back in Sussex. The Swan Sanctuary took over from us at Dale Fort Field Centre. But the repercussions of my two weeks helping those oiled birds in Wales were to have quite a profound effect on my career.

We had received national and international news coverage. Gary and I had been interviewed dozens of times and there had been a lot of local coverage as well.

This all resulted in an increase in the number of phone calls I was receiving from people wanting me to help them with sick, injured and orphaned wildlife. I became so busy I would be frequently leaving work and then doing volunteer wildlife rescues late into the night.

It was at this point that Robin Hooper, from Downwood Vets in Horam, made me an offer I couldn't refuse. I had run up over £1000 in vet's bills and was struggling to repay it. Robin took me aside and suggested that I call a public meeting and set myself up as a voluntary group, with a committee, fundraising events and asking volunteers to help out. This, he suggested, would make it easier to pay the vet's bills and to treat more casualties. He then offered to halve my vet's bill to £500 if I managed it.

He threw down the challenge, and I picked it up.

Within a few weeks I had written over 500 letters, bought 500 stamps, and posted them to various people who had called me out for assistance over the past few years. I set up a meeting in one of the committee rooms at Hailsham Leisure Centre, and some forty of those who had received my letter came along and offered their support, and more crucially, their help.

And so on in September 1996 East Sussex Wildlife Rescue changed from being just me, to a voluntary group, and the first accounts were set up. WRAS, Wildlife Rescue Ambulance Service was on its way.

I then contacted Janet Russell, the head of the arts department at Hailsham Secondary School, and we set about organising a competition to develop a logo for WRAS. It was open to all the students in her art classes as well as the public. A few weeks later we had a winner, fourteen year old Mark Wheeler. He had come up with the simple but effective design of a spiky hedgehog, and our logo, WRAS, underneath. I still treasure the photo of me presenting Mark with £50 worth of vouchers standing next to my new (well, second hand) Ford Escort Estate car on the side of which was Mark's logo and the sign, "Wildlife Ambulance".

I started helping out with fox rescue work at Bexhill. They were also involved in attending demonstrations at Fox Hunts, the live animal exports from Shoreham Harbour, and at the monkey farm at Small Dole. I went to some demos, but because of my rescue work I found it difficult to attend many. I also attended a couple of fox hunts but didn't really know what I was doing to be honest, so found myself quickly left behind and not contributing much. One of my first demonstrations was at Shoreham Harbour against live animal exports. I still can't believe this has not been

60

banned from all ports. I was expecting it to be full of youths wearing black hoods and hiding their faces, but was amazed at how many women and elderly were there. The spirit was great and generally the people were really nice.

Around the same time a couple of the hunt protestors contacted me to say they had word of a hunt about to take place near Heathfield. A woman had apparently called in the local hunt after her chickens had been taken, and they were due to go through the local woodland and try to get rid of the foxes. I was asked if I would attend, from a wildlife rescue perspective, in case they had any injured foxes which needed dealing with. I was on-call from our ambulance parked in a layby. I decided to go for a walk across one of the fields with a couple of the protestors. As we walked past a dilapidated field shelter, we suddenly noticed something underneath it. For all we knew the building had collapsed years ago, but underneath was a fully grown adult sheep. We shouted across the field for some people to help us lift the heavy tiled roof off the ground. This allowed me to crawl underneath and check the sheep. I couldn't feel any spinal injuries and it was moving all four legs, so I slowly and carefully managed to pull it out - not an easy task. Once we had the sheep free from the building, I moved my ambulance to the field gate and unloaded its contents into a friend's car to make room for the sheep. We carefully carried it to the van and I drove it straight to the vets. It turned out that the sheep had been extremely lucky and only had a bruised spine. Not knowing who the farmer was we contacted the Kit Wilson Trust at Hadlow Down who kindly took her in. She ended up living there for the rest of her life and turned into a very handsome and popular resident.

Over the next few years numerous people came and went from our fledgling organisation, but bit by bit we developed and grew, and step by step, found our feet getting stronger and stronger.

I would like to take this opportunity to thank some of those who gave me invaluable support in those early years of WRAS and still continue to do so.

Yvonna at East Hoathly for all her support; Mike and Vicky at Hailsham who allowed us to have an outside fox rehabilitation pen in their woods, as well

61

as helping with fundraising and storage of fundraising goods. Also Anne and Lorraine in Hailsham, who helped out with rescues and took in casualties when they could.

It also led to two people joining WRAS who were to become long-standing and valuable members of WRAS, Val and Murrae Hume. Val originally joined and started helping out with rescues and fundraising events. She was soon joined by her husband Murrae, a police officer with Surrey Police. Having someone else willing to do night time rescues was such a relief, and meant they didn't all fall on my shoulders. They made a huge difference in our ability to cope and save even more casualties.

Chapter 7 - WRAS and I spread our wings.

In the late 1990s, I was still working full time at Abacus Research in Uckfield doing computer programming. Calls numbers were increasing and every day I would find myself building up a list of calls to deal with as soon as I finished work and then spending hours into the night running round. Frustrated that I had to work, and needing more and more help dealing with call-outs, I held a meeting to recruit yet more volunteers. One of them, Julie, became a great friend and has remained so ever since. She's a very passionate and caring animal welfare campaigner.

Julie introduced me to her friend, Lindy, and before long I was renting a room from her in Peacehaven. This saw WRAS's first small scale hospital get off the ground. In Lindy and Julie I found like-minded friends, as passionate about wildlife and its welfare as I was. We had some amazing times and I gained a lot in confidence.

In Lindy's spare room we established a small rescue unit equipped with bird cages and hutches. Lindy and I would take turns to do the night feeds of animals such as fox cubs, so that we could both get enough sleep.

In August 1999 I was contacted by Terry Hill, a Water Processing Technician for Southern Water at Hailsham Water Treatment Works. A swan had crash-landed into one of the treatment tanks and was swimming round and round in circles. As soon as staff spotted the swan they turned off the machinery so the swan didn't become exhausted. This was the first of several such rescues at Hailsham and Uckfield Water Treatment Works. Swans would crash land in the tanks which were too small for them to be able to take off and fly out. The swan at Hailsham was nicknamed Bronson after actor Charles Bronson, who was staring in the Death Wish films.

In the summer of 1999 I was contacted by a market research company in London. The computer software that I was trained to programme was beginning to be phased out. This meant that most market research companies did not want to spend money on training new staff, but rather poach trained staff where possible. As a result, I was offered double my salary to work in London. Desperately in need of the money I took the job, not quite realising the long hours I would have to work and the negative impact this would have on my rescue work. I tried my best to work things around my job and get other volunteers to take on the rescues but it was a struggle.

I would leave Peacehaven at 5am or earlier and drive to Haywards Heath or Lewes where I would catch one of the first trains to London. If you've ever had to change trains at Clapham Junction you will know how long it takes to get from one platform to another. My train would arrive at platform 14, one side of the station, and I would have to run to the far side in order to catch my connecting train to Willesden Junction from platform 1. This was scheduled to leave only 5 minutes after my arriving train. Any delays and I would often see it pulling out of the station as I ran towards the platform. Once at Willesden Junction I walked to the office and after being stuck in the lift four times in the first month I decided I would start using the stairs as a keep fit regime.

The job was great at first but quickly I realised that the clients were not the nicest people and I just wasn't getting on with the management. I loved the programming and problem solving but dealing with the clients was a nightmare. Everything had to be perfect and was always needed yesterday. On one occasion I had a client screaming down the phone at me saying my average figures were wrong, when what they actually wanted was a mean score.

I think while most of us strive to do as well as we can at any given task, very few, if any of us are perfect. I don't believe in perfection and think it wrong to expect it. But sadly we seem to be moving more and more into a society which expects perfection without a single mistake. Even small mistakes are treated like minor crimes by some. I believe we should have the patience and understanding to appreciate that things sometimes go wrong. These days my philosophy is not to get very excited or have high expectations, so I'm not disappointed when something doesn't work out. But when something does go well, then I feel justified in being very pleased with the achievement.

The last train to leave Willesden Junction to catch my connection home at Clapham Junction was about 7.30pm. If I missed this, I would end up

Above "Fred" one of the many pets in Trevor's family. Below Left: Trevor with his mum and Sam the dog at the cliffs at Birling Gap. Below Right: A very young Trevor with a young Sam the dog.

Above: Downland Ranger Alan Ferguson instructs a Dew Pond Restoration Task near East Dean. Below: Trevor (left) helps haul a large bag of rubbish up the cliff for disposal after a day clearing rubbish at Cow Gap near Beachy Head, Eastbourne.

Above Left: The wall of concrete covering the wildlife haven at Summerhill. Above Right: Members of Environment Hailsham at the derelict Grovelands Farm. Below: Trevor in Hailsham Common Pond cleaning out rubbish.

Above: Trevor's emergency newt rescue at Hailsham. Below Left: Meta treats another oiled Guillemot from Seaford Beach. Below Right: One of the toad tunnels near Steyning.

Above Left: Vet Robin Hooper examines a road casualty Squirrel. Above Right: Trevor's first car allows him to check out a Toad Patrol sight at Maresfield. Below: Trevor (right) sets off on a 100km cycle ride to raise money for East Sussex Wildlife Rescue in 1997.

Above: Trevor and Gary Tredwell treat an oil covered guillemot at the Sea Empress Oil Spill in Millford Haven in 1996. Below: British Divers Marine Life Rescue attempt to capture oil covered birds in Millford Haven.

Above Left: Lindy feeds two young thrushs. Above Right: New WRAS volunteers Julie and Murrae help with a swan rescue at Lewes Pells Pond. Below: A concussed road casualty fox which Trevor cared for at his home in Hailsham.

Above: Trevor's first live dolphin stranding of an Atlantic White Sided Dolphin which stranded on Newhaven's West Breach. Below: A photo of the Daily Mail report on the Monkton Marshes Swan Disaster showing hundreds of dead swans beneath the power cables.

Daily Mail, Friday, January 17, 2003

Almost 200 swans die after flying into unmarked power cables

The killing fields

STREWN across a field the swans lie, dead or dying.

Their wings and necks were broken when they flew into power cables slung between pylons.

Almost 200 of the majestic birds have come crashing to earth near the village of Monkton, Kent, this winter. Some lay injured and starving for weeks in ditches before passing rail commuters first raised the alarm in November.

Animal rescue workers have condemned electricity company Seeboard

By **Tim Utton**

for failing to respond to requests to fit reflective markers on the high-voltage lines which would enable the swans to see and avoid them.

The swans fly from a reservoir where they live to the field to feed. They are not hurt by the 132,000 volts passing through the cables, because they are not earthed when they touch them. But the impact breaks their bones.

Trevor Weeks, of East Sussex Wildlife Rescue, said: 'It is horrific to see so

many of these beautiful birds massacred. It is corporate vandalism.'

Stephen Knight, trustee of the Surrey Swan Sanctuary at Egham, which is treating a dozen survivors, said: 'Seeboard have told us it will be at least ten weeks before markers can be placed. How many more will die?'

The power lines, supplying the Isle of Thanet, will have to be shut down for the work to be done. Seeboard originally scheduled it for April to avoid cutting off homes in winter, but said it was now trying to speed things up.

Survivor: An injured bird at the Egham sanctuary

Above Left: A photo of the Argus Newspaper which closely followed the Saltdean Badger Demonstrations. Above Right: Trevor with a baby fox rescued under floor boards in Hastings 2002 and successful reunited with it mum. Below Left: Trevor with a road casualty Badger at the Emergency Vets in Brighton 2002. Below Right: Trevor works with the Fire Service to free a trapped gull on a roof in Peacehaven.

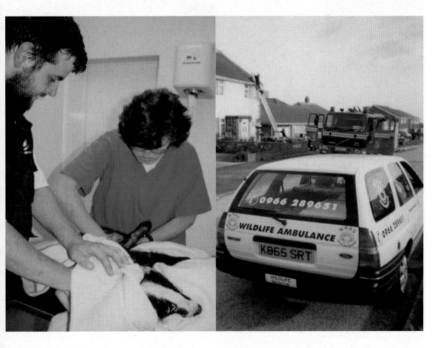

Above: Trevor and Alec rapidly try to free a deer with its antlers caught in a rope swing at Cross in Hand in Heathfield. Below: Trevor's first baby seal rescued on Newhaven West Beach and taken to the RSPCA at East Winch in Norfolk.

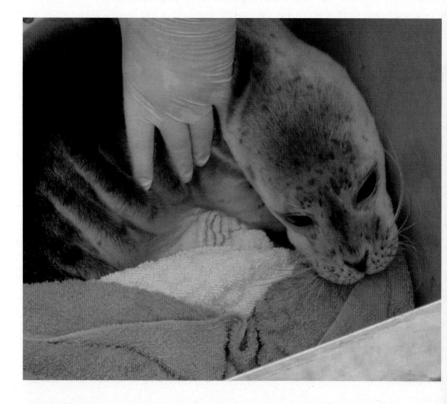

Above Left: Trevor giving lectade to a young fox cub injured by a cat. Above Right: A baby hedgehog being hand reared by Trevor at Peacehaven. Below: Two of the draft photos featuring Trevor for the "Fox Hunting" theme page of the calendar.

Above: A juvenile squirrel trapped in a squirrel proof feeder in Hellingly, which Trevor was called out to rescue. Luckily the squirrel freed itself as Trevor approached. Below: Trevor co-ordinators a major swan rescue at Hove Lagoon in 2004 after the was drained and several swans injured.

Above: The Westham Wall constructed to keep a fighting family of Canadian Geese and Swan apart. Constructed by Trevor and fellow rescuers Alec and Dave in 2005. Below Left: Trevor holding a young seal for tube feeding at BDMLR's Seal Hospital in Scotland. Below Right: Trevor looking for the fox in the Phone Shop Roof (Photo Courtesy of The Argus Newspaper.)

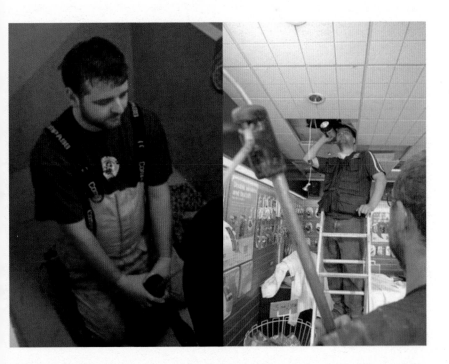

Above: Trevor with Marra the bottlenose dolphin being taken out for release in the Solway Firth after being trapped in Maryport Marina in Cumbria. Below: Trevor was flown to Skegness as part of a rescue team seen here being briefed prior to a rescue attempt, with the helicopter on the beach in the background.

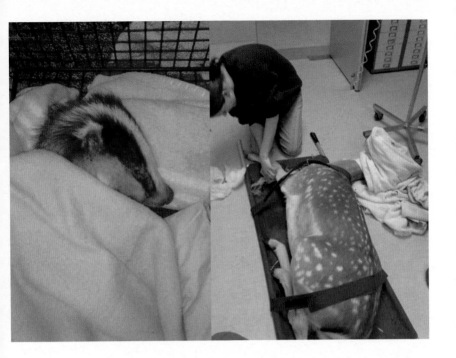

Above Left: Snug and warm all wrapped up this badger was hit on the road at Newhaven. Above Right: An adult Fallow Stag which Trevor drove up to St Tiggywinkles Wildlife Hospital in Buckinghamshire being attended to by one of their nurses. Below Left: Rescuer Maz with an oiled Guillemot at Saltdean. Below Right: Kathy with a dog attacked Swan found out on the Pevensey Levels with a serious wound on the wing.

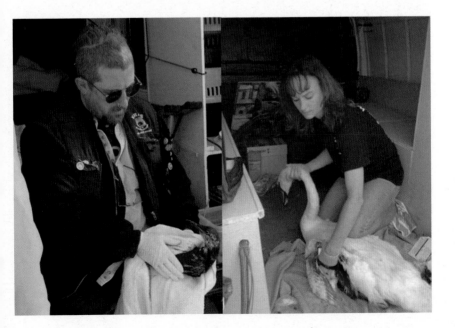

Above: Trevor with the rescued Pheasant which spent 3 hours inside Newhaven B&Q. Picture here with staff from B&Q and the local Fire Service who called out WRAS. Below: The Hayling Island Whale Rescue attempt which Trevor tried to co-ordinate.

spending the night on the office floor. This happened quite regularly. I grew more and more tired working such long hours and in what little time I had at home, I was so exhausted that I couldn't do much. My voluntary work suffered and I started to hate working in London. A £32,000 a year salary was one thing but it did bring happiness. At my six month review they decided to continue my probationary period. This was the last straw, and within the month I had handed in my notice.

They tried to make me work my 3 months' notice until I pointed out the terms of my contract which stated that during my probationary period I only had to give two weeks' notice. I was very lucky to be asked back to Abacus Research. They couldn't offer me London salaries but did offer me my old salary but for less hours, working four days a week. This suited me fine and allowed me to really develop my rescue work.

Over the following two years that I stayed with Abacus, my rescue work picked up big time, although not always in a positive way. During 2001 on two occasions I found myself literally stuck in my ambulance. My back had locked up, and paramedics had to be called to get me out. It was extremely painful and landed me in hospital. The doctors were unsure of the cause, but agreed that I needed to be very careful about how I sat at a desk. My posture, table height, level of the computer screen and long working hours sitting still without moving much were not helping. I was signed off by my doctor for six months. He was very supportive and encouraged me to continue being active and moving around as much as possible, and that I should continue with my rescue work as it kept my back mobile. Despite this, I had no choice but to limit what rescues and activities I undertook. Whatever the cause, I have been plagued by intermittent back pain ever since. Eventually it led to my employers terminating my contract and I lost my job.

I had no choice but to sign on as unemployed, but made a point of asking if I could continue my voluntary work to help me back into employment.

In April 2001 I was called to Newhaven West Beach. A member of the public had reported a huge mud slide which took with it several Fulmars. We went to investigate, but were unable to find any of the birds caught by the mud.

That spring had been an excessively wet one and the rain had caused several chalk falls along other parts of the coast. I was only aware of three sites in East Sussex where these birds were nesting, and the cliffs by Newhaven Fort and West Beach was one of them. Fulmars are often mistaken for gulls, but when you take the time to look at them closely, they are fantastic. On the top of their beaks they have two prominent, tubular nostrils, unlike other birds that have nostrils inside the upper beak. Fulmars are monogamous, re-joining their mates each year at the same nest site, on a rocky ledge, where they lay only one egg per year.

Fulmar chicks have a clever and very effective method of warding off predators. They bring up a stinking oily substance from their stomachs and squirt it in an accurately aimed jet. They also have, unlike most other species of bird, an extremely well-developed sense of smell, which enables them to smell fish oil when out hunting for prey.

In February 2002 I was back in touch with Alan Knight, whom I'd met at the Sea Empress Oil Spill back in 1996, and he invited me to go on their Marine Mammal Medic Training Course. On Sunday 21st April I attended the day long course at Bewl Water. I was very nervous, it was like going back to school, and I didn't know whether there would be an exam or anything at the end.

The morning was spent listening to lectures from BDMLR's directors, Alan Knight and Mark Stevens. In the afternoon everyone changed into wet and dry suits and took part in three practical sessions. The first was how to catch a seal. Using a life size model of a seal pup, we were shown how to jump a seal and secure it using a towel muzzle. The next practical was how to provide first aid to a stranded dolphin, and how to re-float it back into the water, if it was considered healthy enough. The third practical was how to use the whale flotation pontoons. It was a long day, but certainly a memorable one and I learnt a lot. I didn't have to undertake a dreaded exam, and I was now officially a Marine Mammal Medic.

Less than two months later, on the 15th June, as people were celebrating England beating Demark 3-0 in the World Cup quarter finals, I found myself on my way to Newhaven West Beach to investigate a report of real live dolphin stranding. Graham from the Southdowns' Badger Group had called me out, and luckily I was not too far away. I arrived on site and we cleared the area around the dolphin, which turned out to be an Atlantic White Sided Dolphin.

The tide was on its way out and the dolphin had stranded high up, close to the car park wall. I put into action my recent training. I covered the dolphin with wet sheets, dug holes to relieve pressure on the dolphin's pectoral fins, and set up a chain gang to carry water up and keep the dolphin wet.

I spoke to Alan Knight at BDMLR and requested additional assistance. I decided to ring the Fire Service and ask if they could help pump water up to the beach, which they kindly did. Once all the first aid measures were in place, I left Lindy and Julie to keep the dolphin safe and wet and I started my examination and assessment of the animal. The animal's lumbar muscle was in good condition, and its reflexes were working, both of which were hopeful signs.

When Alan arrived he found the fire service, the RNLI and police on site helping to deal with the situation. The beach had been closed to the public and cordoned off for safety. We called a vet to attend, and started trying to figure out what had happened and why the dolphin had stranded. Members of the public had reported seeing the dolphin head-butting the harbour wall when the tide was in and swimming round in tight circles. Although the general assessment of the dolphin showed it to be in good condition, Alan was worried about its behaviour prior to stranding, and the fact that this pelagic species was normally found well off-shore in deep water, not shallow waters like the English Channel.

After seeking advice from James Barnet, one of the UK's leading cetacean vets, a decision was taken to euthanize the dolphin. There were too many factors implying that there were serious navigational problems.

Before we did this, and after a briefing with rescuers, the RNLI and Fire Service, I had the job of breaking the news to the public. Several of them were not happy at first, but once I explained the situation they seemed to understand. I don't like seeing any wildlife casualty being put down, but there are times when it is in the best interest of the animal, and that is what should always be paramount.

Generally, when a dolphin strands it is not good news and is usually due to injury or illness. On this occasion a post mortem examination showed our Newhaven dolphin to have a type of bacterial brain infection. This would have prevented the dolphin from being able to navigate, and certainly it would not have been able to survive had it been released back to the wild.

The members of the public who helped were great, and the team work which went on during the rescue was as good as it can get.

A couple of years later we were called to a common dolphin stranded on the beach at Lancing. It was very old, had very few teeth and was clearly in a very poor condition and sadly also had to be euthanized.

Some people see such outcomes as a failure, but should relieving such suffering be thought of as a failure? I see it more of a success, as we have prevented that animal from suffering a potentially drawn out and horrible death. Surely that has to be a success when there are no other options?

Another rescue, which saw me spreading my wings further afield, was in January 2003. I had a call from Dot and Steve, at the Swan Sanctuary, asking if I would meet them at Monkton Marshes in Kent. This is right up on the southern edge of Thanet, not far from Ramsgate. There had been reports of numerous dead and injured swans in a field.

When I arrived, Steve was already on site and in the process of catching several swans which had broken wings, fractured legs, or de-gloved necks, (where the skin has been completely peeled back like a glove). Around us were hundreds of dead swans, in varying degrees of decomposition, from skeletons to those freshly dead and still warm.

It was a scene of carnage. There were overhead power cables that most likely had been the cause of all the damage, yet this had never occurred here before. But now was not the time to ask why; the swans needed to be rescued, and where possible, treated. We worked with Steve and the Swan Sanctuary volunteers, checking the surrounding drainages ditches and managing to round up several injured swans. These we placed into swan bags, and that night Steve drove back to his sanctuary at Egham where they were treated.

I agreed to stay on, but it wasn't until the evening that I realised I had not picked up my duvet and pillows before leaving home, so had no choice but to bed-down in the ambulance, using the animal blankets and towels. The local pub, The Dog and Duck, let me stay in their overflow car park. Being January, it was extremely cold, and I was driving an old county paramedic ambulance which had been re-signed "Wildlife Ambulance". There was certainly plenty of room for me to lie down, but the draughts coming in from the rear doors were not pleasant.

My role was to be present first thing in the morning and last thing at night to deal with any swans which collided with the power cables. Every day I would be there looking for any injured swans and was trying to work out what on earth had caused this tragedy. We quickly came to realise that the problem resulted from an unusual combination of factors.

It became apparent that this was the first time the local farmer had planted oil seed rape in the fields next to the high voltage electricity pylons. The swans seemed to be spending the night on a nearby reservoir, and then grazing on the oil seed rape fields during the day. The swan's flight path, from reservoir to rape fields, took them over the top of the intervening wooded railway line. This was the same height as the power cables, so the swans then had to negotiate them in order to land in the fields of oil seed rape.

The Swan Sanctuary contacted Seeboard, the local electricity company, and discovered they had been aware of the problem since the early winter, but had decided it would be impossible to get the right sort of machinery on the land in order to place bird diverters on the cables.

Whilst I was patrolling the fields every morning and evening, Steve at the Swan Sanctuary was working on encouraging Seeboard to take action. At first they were not very keen, so Steve contacted the local television news and local newspapers who were rapidly on site and covering the incident. Even the Daily Mail printed an article.

After about 10 days of campaigning, we were visited by the Environmental Officer from Seeboard. He said that they were looking at the possibility of bringing machinery onto the site and lowering the cables to the ground so that bird diverters could be attached along three spans of the cables.

I lived on site for just over two weeks, and during my stay seven swans hit the cables and needed rescuing. It was horrendous not being able to do anything to stop it from happening. I would stand at the edge of the field waiting, holding my breath, willing them to clear the cables as they flew in. My heart would race as I quickly ran across the field when a collision occurred, getting to the swan as soon as possible to be able to help it.

After a lot of planning, Seeboard were able to bring in machinery to start work on the cables. This involved re-routing electricity to half the households in Thanet. It was a major undertaking which took most of the day. Steve and I paid tribute to Seeboard in the press for finding a solution to the problem, but it was a shame so many swans had to die before they would take action. This was the first time bird diverters had been used on high voltage cables in Kent.

I stayed on for a few more days after the work had taken place to ensure no further swans were injured, and luckily the bird diverter disks seemed to work. At the end of my stay what had originally been a flock of over two hundred and twenty swans had been reduced to less than twenty.

Chapter 8 - It's not always Black and White.

One Friday, in late 2002, I received a phone call from Elaine King the CEO of the National Federation of Badger Groups (now the Badger Trust). She told me that the Department of Environment Food and Rural Affairs (DEFRA) had issued a licence to trap and kill up to 14 badgers living in a sett in the back gardens of some houses in Saltdean. According to the information given to Elaine, the gable end of one of the properties was at risk of collapsing because the ground was being undermined by the badgers and their sett. Elaine explained that there were claims that their gardens were being taken over by the badgers, that they were causing hundreds of pounds worth of damage, and that previous attempts at resolving the problem had failed.

Shortly after this I was contacted by a local resident, whose house overlooked the gardens, who told me that traps had already been set on and around the badger sett.

Like a shot I was on my way to Saltdean. I contacted Elaine at the Badger Federation who immediately started making calls and enquiries. She was supposed to have been told in advance if traps were being placed.

I also alerted the local media, and various other organisations, hoping to drum up support for a demonstration. Within a couple of hours a small group of people, armed with banners, had gathered on the pavement outside the affected properties protesting about the cull. We did not know exactly which houses were the licence holders, so had no choice but to stand on the main verge at the base of a U shaped section of roads and houses that surrounded the sett.

Saltdean, like Peacehaven and other towns that had sprung up after the war, had been built without much regard for the presence of badger setts and, as a result, a number of houses ended up with badgers living underneath them or in their basements.

Other setts in the area had already been closed down by DEFRA, which meant that they were then forced to move elsewhere. In the licence application for these particular houses it was claimed that previous attempts to exclude the badgers had been unsuccessful, so there was no alternative but to cull them.

However, I was informed by one of the people involved in this exclusion attempt, the reason the exclusion had failed was because the residents did not maintain the cordon, leaving gates open and allowing the badgers to return. I was also told that there was no way the gable ends of any of the properties would be affected by the tunnels going under the foundations of the houses.

Generally a badger's tunnel is formed in a D shape with the flat edge of the D to the ground. They are not normally wider than 30cm and when they go under foundations at right angles, a tunnel that size and shape is not a risk to the property.

A small group of local people had started gathering along the pavement and soon the police arrived. They asked questions and warned us that any breach of the peace would not be tolerated. I made it clear that our intention was for the demonstration to be peaceful and non-violent. I also told the police that I would not leave the site until the traps had been removed.

With the help of Karen Hoy, a reporter at the Argus Newspaper, our story became front page news for several days in a row. It also hit the headlines on the BBC South East news. By Saturday afternoon well over five hundred people had turned up to demonstrate outside the residents' homes. Despite being called "rent-a-mob" by the licence holders, those who attended were a mixture of local residents and animal lovers from further afield. Both young and old came from far and wide to support our protest against the cull. I was approached by a group of animal rights activists, and I explained to them that this was to be a peaceful demonstration and that people-power would win. They respected this and said if we needed them they would step in.

Later that day The Badger Federation received confirmation from DEFRA that traps had been put on-site, and that two badgers had already been caught and shot. I felt sick at the thought that they had managed to kill them, and having been up most of the night was exhausted and emotional and reduced to tears. That night I slept in a deckchair on the grass verge and the support I had was amazing. There can only have been about two hours when I was on my own, the rest of the time I had people there supporting me.

On Sunday there was again another large group of residents with banners and signs campaigning against the badger cull. It was very heart-warming to see so many people coming along. One guy felt so sorry for us that he even pulled up in his car with a much welcome delivery of pizzas.

Over the weekend Solicitor, Matthew Gold, worked on behalf of the Badger Federation and drew up plans for a Judicial Review.

Generally the police were sympathetic and understanding, although we did experience the odd officer who was a bit of a 'jobs worth' and clearly felt intimidated by our presence. Chief Inspector Peter Mills visited on the Sunday and expressed his concerns over long-term policing the demonstration, and what it would take to resolve it. The simple answer, I told him, was that we would leave as soon as the traps were removed. CI Mills contacted Elliot Morley, the Environment Minister at DEFRA, and persuaded him to order the removal of the traps and for DEFRA to start a discussion with the National Federation of Badger Groups to resolve the situation without the need for a badger cull.

By Monday morning I was extremely tired, having had less than eight hours sleep since the Friday morning when I had first been alerted to the situation. Then I received a phone call from Sussex Police's Wildlife Crime Officer saying that the traps were going to be removed and he would be arriving that afternoon to do so.

In front of a group of about a hundred demonstrators the traps were removed by the police, put in a van and taken away. I was shown into the garden to see for myself that the traps had gone, and at this point one of the residents started shouting and screaming out of the window telling me to "get off my ******** land." Very pleasant!

With the removal of the last trap, a bottle of champagne was opened and we celebrated our success. I spoke to the crowd, thanking them for their support and for being so well behaved.

CI Peter Mills later told me that this had been one of the most well behaved demonstrations he had attended, and that was the reason he decided to step in and contact DEFRA on our behalf to get the traps removed.

This wasn't the end of the situation though. Over the following weeks Elaine King visited the site and a survey was done of the area mapping out badger activity. The affected gardens were also surveyed. With the help of Professor Steven Harris of Bristol University, a report was written for DEFRA and a potential solution proposed.

I was rather out of my depth here and my knowledge of badgers was limited, so had to bow to everyone else's experience and knowhow. Like everyone I wasn't prepared to walk away without seeing the situation resolved.

The report concluded that the systematic destruction of badger setts in the area had left the local badger population with very few remaining, which is why this particular sett was so large and heavily used. It stated that the gardens were on the last remaining sections of an historic lynchet, giving the badgers a nice deep layer of earth to dig into and form a sett.

A lynchet is a bank of earth across a sloping hillside. They are caused by soil that has built up on the downslope of a field ploughed over a long period of time. They are common features seen in ancient field systems across the South Downs.

Across most of Saltdean the soil depth is very shallow before you hit hard chalk, which is not suitable for badgers to dig into.

Professor Harris proposed that two artificial setts should be created in neighbouring gardens and dug into the bed rock chalk so the badgers could not extend it. Then the sett currently causing the problem could be closed without the badgers being homeless, and those gardens should be badger-proofed to stop them from trying to build another sett there.

Eventually DEFRA agreed to this plan and funded the work which successfully took place the following year, much to everyone's relief, without the need to cull any further badgers.

It is amazing what you can achieve with public support, and there is no doubt that badgers provoke a passion in the public not achieved by many other wild animals.

Over the years I encountered situations where I have really had to debate what the best course of action to take is, and in some cases the decisions are really never that clear. Take for example birds caught in netting on buildings. People erect netting over buildings to stop birds perching or nesting, and as a result they become entangled. Under the Animal Welfare Act once a wild animal or bird becomes caught up, and the owner of the property is aware of the situation, then the owner has a legal responsibility to ensure the five freedoms apply as the animal or bird is now captive.

The five freedoms are:

1.   Freedom from hunger or thirst by ready access to fresh water and a diet to maintain full health and vigour

2.   Freedom from discomfort by providing an appropriate environment including shelter and a comfortable resting area

3.   Freedom from pain, injury or disease by prevention or rapid diagnosis and treatment

4.   Freedom to express (most) normal behaviour by providing sufficient space, proper facilities and company of the animal's own kind

5.   Freedom from fear and distress by ensuring conditions and treatment which avoid mental suffering

If the entrapped bird isn't dealt with, within a reasonable period of time, the owner of the building could then be prosecuted. For years I attended virtually all of the call-outs to ensnared birds. We helped free them, treat them, rehabilitate them where possible and release them back to the wild, but rarely would we see any donation from the owner, letting agent, or resident of the building. Generally these birds are caught because of the way in which the netting has been erected or because it has not been maintained. There are several sites where we have been called out repeatedly to deal with entangled birds, in some cases up to six or more times. Yet, despite asking for the netting to be changed or repaired it rarely gets done, leading to more and more birds being caught.

How do you get such people to change their attitude, and prevent birds suffering long term? We tried saying that we would have to charge them if we got called out more than three times, but they would just say they would call out pest control to shoot it. We've tried telling members of the public who see entangled birds to speak to the building owner directly, and tell them that they have a legal responsibility under the Animal Welfare Act to deal with it, and if they don't then they could be prosecuted. This then leads to members of the public criticising us for not attending, when their aggression and anger should really be aimed at the people who have caused the birds to become caught up. What is better; attending every entangled bird event and spending our limited resources in dealing with them, sometimes repeatedly in the same place, or do we take a stand and let one suffer in order to prevent dozens of others from suffering? It's a really difficult balance to achieve.

In cases where the owner of the property can't be contacted or when the property owner contacts us direct asking for assistance with a trapped bird, then we try our best to step in and help.

We are contacted by members of the public all the time asking us to take action to prevent an animal or bird from suffering. A common example is reports of dogs left in cars in the heat. Under the law, you can't break in and stop the dog from becoming hot and suffering: you have to wait till the dog is suffering before taking action.

The Animal Welfare Act has made it easier for organisations like the RSPCA to step in and give advice in an attempt to prevent suffering, but this can still only be done if one of the five freedoms has been breached. The ambiguous wording of the Countryside and Wildlife Act, as well as other animal welfare legislation, is often difficult to interpret and use, especially where there is no case law to guide a prosecution.

Many people like to "rescue" animals from people or pet stores by buying them and providing a good home for them. While this may stop a particular animal from suffering, does it not then encourage the breeder or pet store owner to continue to breed and sell more animals which then suffer? So you end up encouraging the suffering of animals by doing so. It's far from straightforward.

It is my belief that Animal Welfare legislation needs to be stronger, and measures should be put in place to help prevent suffering and allow those in authority to be pro-active in preventing suffering.

I also strongly believe that nobody should be allowed to keep, let alone breed from, any living creature without being qualified to do so first. Too many people have pets because of the status of the breed or species, or because of the latest craze. Owning an animal is a huge responsibility and if you can't afford to look after or keep an animal properly then you shouldn't have it in the first place. This is a view which seems so obvious to me, yet it's one that has caused a number of arguments.

Chapter 9 - A leap of faith.

WRAS was now dealing with over 2000 calls for help a year. As our work grew and we became more well known, we found ourselves getting called to more and more different species of wildlife. In 2003 we dealt with our first deer rescue. It was a roe deer that had been caught in an iron gate at the side of a house at Haywards Heath. When we arrived the deer was on the ground and had managed to get her head and front legs between two bars of the gate but was unable to get her pelvis through. We came to the conclusion that the deer must have encountered a near miss, or glancing blow from a car on the road, and in trying to escape, had run at full pelt towards the gate and got stuck.

We covered the deer's head to help keep her calm. We tried pushing the bars apart, but they were just too thick. We had no choice but to ask for assistance from the Fire Service. Within minutes a fire engine with flashing blue lights arrived from Hayward's Heath fire station. It was clear that the gate was going to need cutting and, with permission from the owner, they set about it.

After the bars had been cut, we gently lifted the deer and released her from the gate. It was clear that we could not immediately release her, but who should I call? I rang round several organisations but none were able to help. Out of desperation I contacted the Swan Sanctuary at Egham and asked them if they knew of anyone. Having contacted St Tiggywinkles, the wildlife hospital in Buckinghamshire, who gave them advice, the Swan Sanctuary agreed to take in the deer and constructed a makeshift pen for her. We were delighted when, after two weeks of care, they rang us to say that the deer was ready to be released. We drove back to the Swan Sanctuary to collect her, took her back to Hayward's Heath where we released her in the woodland on the opposite side of the road to where she was found. This was a first for WRAS and one which was to be repeated quite a few times at various locations.

Over the next ten years we found ourselves dealing with numerous deer casualties. Several of these were road casualties and we took them to the Kit Wilson Trust or the Sussex Horse Rescue Trust, but virtually every one of them had suffered spinal damage, and had to be put to sleep. Sadly we found that most vets were not prepared to help us deal with these road casualties especially out of hours. On one occasion, when a deer had been struck by a car and paralysed on the A22 at Maresfield, it took four hours to get a vet out to help us. This led us to question whether what we were doing was fair on the deer. Sitting there with it that night for hours on end and watching it suffer with no means of being able to help it was truly horrible.

That same year saw us called to a deer with its antlers caught in a rope swing at Heathfield. This was another first for me and I was nervous to say the least. A new rescuer, Alec, was helping me and we took with us blankets, cutting equipment and a new "walk-towards" net. This looks like a tennis court net strung between two metal poles. It's a piece of equipment that doesn't come cheap. They cost over £100 each, and if the net is broken during the rescue, that's the end of it, as it can't easily be repaired.

As we walked down the field the deer started trying to get away. It would charge away from us and then suddenly flip over onto its back as it reached the end of the rope, then jump up again and run in a different direction and flip over again. It was very upsetting to see, panting away, very exhausted and tired.

Alec and I, holding either end of the net, slowly tried to approach the deer, one on each side of it. This meant that we were being hit by the end of the branch that the rope swing was attached to. Suddenly, the deer tried to run between us and bolted straight into our net. We were then able to pin the deer to the floor and approach safely. I sat astride the deer, keeping it down using some of my body weight. Alec started cutting the rope from the antlers, which were quite badly entangled, while I started removing the "walk-towards" net. The deer had become so entangled in the net that the only way to free him quickly, was to cut it. It would mean £100 down the drain, but at what cost is a deer's life?

After about 13 minutes of working on the deer we were in a position to set him free. Alec backed off first then I leapt backwards, pulling back the blanket to clear it from the deer's head. In horror I watched as the blanket got caught on one of its antlers, and still wearing it, the deer sprinted away across the field. Much to our relief, the deer managed to shake off its ungainly headwear and after a few hundred yards it slowed down, stopped and turned round to look at us, breathing deeply. I like to think the deer was saying "thank you".

These types of rescues, dealing with a healthy deer which is just caught up, are very tricky. From the point of capture to the point of release you have a 30 minute window in which to get the deer free. Any longer than that, it is likely to have a heart attack and die, or be too badly stressed to be released. Despite their size and strength, they are very sensitive animals. This episode led me to find out more about deer rescues from the experts at St Tiggywinkles Wildlife Hospital.

When trying to save and protect wildlife it can sometimes bring you into conflict with people. We often find ourselves between a rock and a hard place. We always try to find a balance, but the animal's welfare has to come first.

As I've mentioned before, swans can arouse very protective and proprietorial emotions in humans. On one such occasion I was asked by the Swan Sanctuary to attend a pair of swans and their cygnets in a drainage ditch in Worthing. It was late in the evening and local residents were concerned for the cygnets which should not be stranded on water overnight without being able to get onto dry land.

It is well recognised that very young, newly hatched cygnets, goslings and ducklings can easily develop hypothermia if they are stuck on water for long periods of time and especially overnight when temperatures drop.

The local animal rescue organisation unfortunately didn't do out of hours rescues so were not available, hence the reason WRAS was called. Under advice from the Swan Sanctuary, we caught the entire family and transported them to a new home where they could live safely.

The swans had been highlighted locally the previous week, after youths had been witnessed throwing stones at them and trying to disturb the nest and eggs. WRAS and local residents had spent several nights visiting them to ensure they stayed safe, because no local animal rescue organisations were available at night or weekends when the main problems were occurring.

This late night rescue unfortunately upset a local Worthing Councillor who contacted the local press and branded me a pirate and said of my midnight mission "I bet Mr Weeks thinks he's a hero but I think he's a bit of a pirate" claiming I should have consulted the council and other rescue organisations before stepping in. Well, I might have if they worked out of hours.

It was a repeat version of the swan rescue at Hailsham, and an attitude I have become very accustomed to over the past thirty years. I do my best to ignore such insults, but still find they can be upsetting.

It always seems to be the way when people feel left out of the loop or aren't in control of a situation that they lash out unnecessarily at people who are just doing the right thing.

There was no way of contacting any relevant person at the council out of hours, nor the local animal rescue organisation, and as there was an immediate risk to the cygnets' lives they had to be rescued. They could not wait for a committee decision which would potentially be too late. We pointed out that we would not be returning the swans as this would be unnecessary stress to them and that they were now in a new location which was safer and better than the drainage ditch full of shopping trolleys and rubbish. It was sad that we had to remind the council that they do not own the swans and they are not council property.

I have never and would never catch any wild animal or birds just for the sake of it. I would rather spend my time, energy and money dealing with those who do really need help. I can't afford to waste money and resources. When I train rescuers, I teach them to assess each situation on its own merit, as no two situations are ever the same. I am always happy to give advice over the phone, but the final decision is always down to the person on site who can see the entire situation for themselves and they are always the best person to make the right decision.

The Swan Sanctuary also asked us to get involved in another late night rescue at the Brooklands Lake at Lancing. Once again nobody could get hold of the local animal rescue service, so Murrae and I drove across. West Sussex Fire Brigade also attended with their rescue boat from Storrington. Using a spotlight, we were able to corner the very poorly female swan and take it to be treated at the Swan Sanctuary in Shepperton, at least an hour's drive away. We finally got home at about 3am. Just over a week later, we heard that the local animal rescue service had caught and removed the cob swan which was found to be virtually dead on arrival at the vet's.

Dot Beeson, who had recently received the British Empire Medal and was the founder of the Swan Sanctuary, called me and asked if we would catch the rest of the family as she felt the site was unsafe. She told me that the swans were suffering from an extremely virulent form of botulism. The local animal rescue service objected to the swans being removed and even complained to the RSPCA. Dot contacted Her Majesty's Swan Marker, and obtained permission from him to have the swans caught. The remaining six swans were taken to the Swan Sanctuary where they were placed in a quarantine pen. One of the youngsters was not looking very well at all and was placed in the hospital for observation. Luckily the rest of the family looked fine, and they were eventually released at a new site that was free from botulism.

Another example of one of the frustrations we face came in October 2003. I received an e-mail from a lady in Alfriston who had found a hedgehog weighing about 170grams. The lady had decided not to ring WRAS's rescue line but send an e-mail asking for advice. The e-mail had been sent on a Friday and I didn't see it till Sunday. The lady explained that the hedgehog had a wound on its head which had been covered in maggots. They had picked them off and washed the wound with salt water. They then placed the hedgehog in a box with bedding and gave it dog food and milk. I asked if it had been seen by a vet or received any veterinary treatment, to which she replied "No we thought it was going to die".

This attitude has always amazed me. Surely if you think something is going to die, isn't it even more of a reason to get it to the vet's or a rescue organisation? When witnessing a car accident and a fatally injured human, you wouldn't say "I think he is going to die therefore, let's just clean him up and not worry about taking him to the hospital".

Rescuer Lindy went to attend the maggot-infested hedgehog. The smell of the wound was horrendous and, as the hedgehog had not had any antibiotics, the tissue was badly infected. To her horror as she cleaned the wounds, she lifted a flap of skin and loads of maggots appeared. Straight away she phoned the on-call duty vet and rushed the hedgehog in for treatment. Amazingly, after a lot of hard work by Lindy, the hedgehog eventually made a full recovery. There was little doubt that it would have suffered a long and slow death if it had not been taken in when it was. Several people said I should have reported the lady to the RSPCA, but I think she genuinely thought she was doing the right thing and didn't do it out of malice, but more out of ignorance. I was certain that she wouldn't do it again and therefore there was no point in taking it any further. I also did not want to discourage her from calling us in future.

We had an unusual rescue after being called to a house in Southover High Street, Lewes. The householder, Mr Duncan, had been somewhat startled when mid-morning, while working in his study, saw a badger stroll past his office door. It had, apparently, wandered in through the open back door, across the hall, past his study, down some steps and into the shower room. On arrival, we discovered the badger certainly had a rather fragrant odour, though I doubted he'd been having a wash and brush-up. That smell indicated something rather less pleasant. As we opened the door to the shower room, the badger ran to the corner and tried to get under the wall where a piece of board was missing. I managed to grab the badger by the rear in order to stop him disappearing out of reach. This is not something I would normally advise anyone to do. Badgers are extremely strong, with very powerful jaws. We then managed to wrap him in a blanket and put him straight into a badger cage. After a brief examination, we rushed the badger to Meridian Vets at Peacehaven where, under sedation, it was discovered he had a nasty territorial bite wound infested with maggots, hence the fragrant odour. He was cleaned up and the maggots removed - who says our job is nice?

Now you might be mistaken in thinking that this job ended there, but far from it. We knew from the start that the release would be problematic. The badger had clearly got to where he was found by walking along a terraced street. He had then gone through a courtyard gate in order to get to the door of the house. The badger would have had to have walked over three hundred metres along the terraced road to get to the house that he had wandered into. Badgers which have been in territorial fights need to be released as close as possible to where they were found, so they can re-unite with their own social group which will afford some sort of protection. This may well be near another social group, and if the badger is released in the wrong place, which may only be a matter of a few metres away, they may well find themselves at "the wrong end of the street" as it were, and right in the midst of the neighbouring badger group that could potentially beat him up again. So by releasing him up one end of the street onto the Downs, or the other end of the street and out onto the marshes, could result in putting the badger into an area he didn't know, and back in touch with the badgers who attacked him.

We surveyed the area and found a couple of possible badger pathways at either end of the street, but nothing close to the house from which he had been rescued. We decided there was only one thing to do; to release the badger in the middle of the road and let him make the decision himself. We contacted Sussex Police and asked for their assistance. We worked out with them when would be the quietest time of the week at night to shut the road and release the badger.

We went for an early Monday morning at 2am. The police closed Southover High Street at the roundabout by the Swan Inn and at Cockshut Road. Once everyone was in place, we put the cage in the centre of the road where the badger could look around and recognise where it was. After a few minutes I opened the door to the cage, the badger hesitated and then shot out and ran towards Cockshut Road. We initially thought the badger was going to run down towards the marshes but it stopped and went into a garden on the town-centre side of the road. Then it disappeared under a garden gate and that was the last we saw of it.

The following day we returned to investigate the area where we last saw him. This time we discovered a badger route at the back of the gardens leading down to the Winterbourne Stream, which we had not seen previously. Mystery solved and, I hope, badger safely reunited with his group.

Summer 2003 saw us having a bit of fun when one of our supporters suggested we do a calendar. A couple of years earlier the Women's Institute had launched their now notorious "Calendar Girls" with photos of typical WI activities, but featuring naked ladies modestly covered with cats, knitting, cakes and more. We thought we might be able to do something similar, but a little different. Rather than baring all, we wanted to do a play on words. For example, we did a photo called "A Bird caught in netting" which was Lindy wrapped up in netting on a beach. We also had a picture entitled "A Gannet" featuring Christine stuffing her face full of cakes and chocolate. "Going for a duck" with was a cricket theme. "Fox hunting" featured me, dressed in a red jacket and no trousers, being chased by someone in a fox outfit and my trousers in their paw. Another was called "Oiled Birds" with three of our female volunteers' sun bathing on the beach with a drum titled "Crude Oil" and a volunteer rubbing the oil on their backs. "Old Deers" was a photo of two naked people wearing grey wigs, and walking off into the sun set with a walking stick and Zimmer frame. Other photos included - "Where do squirrels hide their nuts", "Swan Lake", "Birds of Prey" and "Easter Bunny". It was a laugh trying to put all the photos together. Unfortunately, although we had quotes before we started the work, to ensure it was going to be affordable, when we went back to the company to get them printed they realised they had not quoted correctly. Suddenly we found the price rocketing well out of our range, and the whole project hit the rocks and collapsed. I still have a copy of the main photos and some of those which didn't make the final calendar, which I occasionally get out for a laugh!

In August 2003, I was called out to a fox at Newhaven. It was a simple rescue and the fox was then taken to Meridian Vets in Peacehaven to be sedated and examined. We would often help the vets at this practice who are very sympathetic towards wildlife. Whilst dealing with the fox, and due to a slight lack of communication, both the vet and I removed our hands from the fox at the same time. The fox swiftly reached round and bit my hand. I managed to regain control of the fox and scruff him again, but it was darned painful - there were certainly a few chosen words spoken.

Once the fox was sorted, I washed my hands, cleaned up the bite wounds and as it was a busy afternoon, jumped straight into my ambulance and drove off to the next rescue. About 10 minutes down the road, I suddenly came over all dizzy, nauseous and sweaty. I pulled over into a bus stop and, feeling very light headed, picked up my phone and called a friend. Then I passed out in the back of my ambulance.

The next thing I knew, I was being woken by paramedics. My blood sugar levels were very low and my early morning start and lack of sleep probably had a lot to do with me passing out. After treatment at Brighton Hospital I was released home again.

Another rescue which ended up with me paying a brief trip to hospital was caused by a pigeon. It was stuck in a flue at the back of a kitchen at the New Europe Hotel on Madeira Drive Brighton. Kitchen staff, who were preparing dinner, heard a noise above the cookers and noticed a pigeon had fallen four floors down the cooker flue. The pigeon was standing on top of an extractor fan and I had to use a small ladder from our ambulance to reach up high enough inside the flue. I was working in darkness and, after reaching through the fan blades, I had to gently manoeuvre the bird between the fan blades and then climb back down the ladder. Although the bird was slightly underweight it was healthy enough and flew off as soon as it was released outside. The kitchen eventually reopened after two hours and cooking resumed, but I ended up having to pop into the Eye Hospital at Brighton after scratching my eye with all the grit and soot in the flue.

Later that year, we attended a major sewage leak in Eastbourne. We had been contacted by local residents and Environment Agency staff at the Shinewater area of Eastbourne. The pollution was believed to have come from a pumping station at Polegate, and then travelled along the dykes to reach the large lakes at Shinewater, located between Langney and Hampden Park, Eastbourne. There were several pairs of swans on the dykes and around Shinewater Park. We attended on site and were able to catch and move them to cleaner water at Princes Park, Eastbourne. Other swans in neighbouring dykes were monitored to ensure they were not affected by the spill. Two swans had also been taken into care by the Swan Sanctuary as they were heavily covered in pollution from the main spill, had digested it and become ill. When incidents like this happen, the Environment Agency put out warnings to the public to keep dogs and pets away from the polluted water, and in rural locations most wildlife will fly off from polluted areas. However if this happens in more residential areas ducks, swans and geese will often stay around. It is thought this is primarily due to the abundance of food, i.e. people feeding bread to the birds. So generally in parks or urban areas where such spillages occur, we will step in and move the swans out of harm's way where possible. Unfortunately trying to catch the ducks is much harder and when you try they will often fly off, away from the affected areas anyway.

The following year we were pleased to see the local authority responsible for the leak were fined by the Environment Agency for the pollution; sadly we never see any of this money to help towards the costs and expenses we incur when dealing with the incident and saving the birds.

In October 2003 we received a call from the emergency vet at Kemp Town asking if we could help them. A dog had fallen 25ft from the top of the undercliff walk onto rocks below. For over an hour the owners tried to get the RSPCA and local vets to help, but had no luck. Out of desperation the emergency vet, realising how stressed the owners were, phoned us to see if we could do anything. Rescuers Lindy, Julie and I drove over to find that the dog had already bitten one of the owners when she had tried to move it. We took heat pads with us to help provide warmth and to reduce the risk of shock. It was crystal clear to us that there was a spinal injury, and without sedation it was highly likely that the dog would suffer more serious injuries. We phoned back the emergency vet with our assessment, but were told that it was the practice policy that he could not leave the surgery building and that emergencies had to be delivered to them. Five minutes later the vet phoned again, and said he was going to break the rules and attend but only had his car, so would we mind transporting the dog to their practice? Well, if the vet was willing to put himself out, then we certainly were too.

The dog was sedated and then carried up the beach to one of WRAS's ambulances. The golden retriever called "Polo" was rushed to the vets and straight into the operating theatre. We later heard that x-rays revealed a fractured leg and spine. Sadly Polo was put to sleep whilst still under sedation.

As I've mentioned, we wouldn't normally deal with domestic pets or farm animals that have owners to look after them, however there are some occasions when you just have to help if you can. This particular vet and his practice had been extremely supportive to WRAS and you could hear in his voice that he was frustrated about not being able to attend and was desperate for help. It was the least we could do.

2003 was a difficult year for me and I was really struggling to cope. I was unemployed and spending so much money on my rescue work I could often only afford a loaf of bread and eating toast. Taking pity on me, Alan Knight offered me a part time job for International Animal Rescue in their offices at Uckfield. I started working there three days a week, but it was enough to keep me afloat and on a better diet. Without Alan's rescue mission on me, I might well have ended up toast myself. I am very grateful.

Chapter 10 - Is this the start of things to come?

At the end of 2003 we received a call concerning wood pigeons. Over one hundred dead ones had been found scattered along a half mile stretch of road to Telscombe village. A walker had stumbled across this apparent slaughter, and was disgusted by what he saw. Motorists had been forced to slow down and swerve around the birds, but many had been squashed under car tires. We examined the birds, and discovered they had been shot. It was a horrendous sight and we contacted the Department of Environment, Food and Rural Affairs (DEFRA) as the dumping of dead animals in this way is a breach of the 1990 Environmental Protection Act.

We suspected that whoever had done this, had shot the birds elsewhere, gathered them up and simply scattered them along the road on some jovial journey home. We just hope they were all dead prior to being strewn along the road. Sadly the culprit was never found.

The beginning of 2004 was a bad year for badgers. In the first couple of months WRAS dealt with fifteen dead, six injured and two emaciated badgers which had been hit by cars. This was about 30% up on all previous years. The number of other road casualties had also increased. These included eleven foxes, five gulls, five deer, three swans, two wagtails, a duck, jackdaw, a pigeon and a dove.

Was this because drivers were getting more careless, or because WRAS was becoming better known, and therefore receiving more calls? Whatever the reason, and I doubt that it was because the animals were getting more careless, we were becoming increasingly busy.

Another first for WRAS in 2004 was a call to a squirrel stuck in a 'squirrel proof' bird feeder. The squirrel had managed to squeeze through the bars of the feeder and get inside and, having eaten his fill of peanuts, was clearly too big to get back out. The incident occurred in Firle Road, Seaford, and I went over to see what I could do to release the now not-so-little chap. I covered the feeder with a small piece of sheeting to try and keep the squirrel calm, and then tried to cut him out. Unfortunately my wire cutters weren't man enough for the tough wire of the feeder. After making several unsuccessful attempts to free the squirrel, I resorted to asking the Fire

Service if they could help provide better cutters. As luck would have it, a crew from Seaford were not far away and arrived within minutes of my call. They were able to cut free the squirrel which happily ran off back to the wild where he could digest his ill-gotten peanuts in peace. During the spring, juvenile squirrels are slightly smaller than adults and it's not uncommon for them to squeeze inside bird feeders, stuff themselves with nuts and then find themselves too fat to get out again. Sometimes just getting close to them is enough to cause them an adrenaline rush that gives them the strength to be able to force their way out, but sometimes they needing cutting free. It was time to buy myself a heftier pair of wire cutters!

About a month later, in May, I again had to call on the Fire Service, this time in Eastbourne. WRAS was called out by staff at the Eastbourne Gazette and Herald newspaper offices, then based in Commercial Road. They were concerned about a gulls' nest on their roof that was blocking the fire safety vent. It was clear that on health and safety grounds a Natural England general licence could be used to remove the nest, but the staff were concerned about what they would do if the gulls had laid eggs or had young. The problem was that the fire safety vent was too high and too far across the roof for me to be able to reach the nest safely. They had already tried several times to get various contractors to come in with machinery to help move the nest, but no one had been available quickly enough and blocking a fire vent was in breach of their fire safety. I suggested contacting the fire service and asking if they could help, but a situation not involving a trapped animal would result in a charge. The manager agreed the charge with the Fire Service and they duly arrived with an aerial platform. They asked me if I would go up and onto the platform and carry out the work. When I reached the roof it was obvious that the nest was not in use, no eggs had been laid and there were no young gulls around. So I cleared away the nest and the fire safety vent was operational again.

In July 2004 I received a call from Pauline Grant who runs the Sussex Horse Rescue Trust at Uckfield. A local thirteen year old lad called Bradley had found a baby fallow deer in the middle of a field. It was out in the open, in short grass land and very exposed. Bradley had picked up the baby deer and had managed to carry it all the way from Buxted Park to the Horse Sanctuary, about a mile. Having phoned me for advice, Pauline had put the deer into the back of their horse-box on a bed of straw. When I arrived I found it was comfortable and calm.

We were so impressed by Bradley that we contacted the local paper. He made front page news on that week's edition of the Sussex Express. Bradley told the Express "At first I thought I would take her back home, but then I asked some passers-by what to do. One man told me just to leave her there, but she was yelping and shaking and I didn't think that was a very good idea. Then another man told me about the Sussex Horse Rescue and I thought someone there would be able to help. I carried her all the way and my arms were aching by the end of it."

The deer was very young, and one of the smallest I had ever dealt with so I phoned Les Stocker at St Tiggywinkles Wildlife Hospital near Aylesbury, Buckinghamshire, and they very kindly agreed to take it on. I had tried local centres that were not able to help on this occasion. It was a long journey, a round trip of almost 200 miles, but well worth it to see their facilities and ensure the youngster would eventually be returned to the wild.

A few months later we had a rather disturbing call from a dog walker. He had found what he described as "two deer with their antlers stuck together, thrashing around and unable to separate". I had never received such a call before and was really unsure of what we were going to face. I asked one of our new volunteers to jump on board and phoned Alan Knight from International Animal Rescue and British Divers Marine Life Rescue. Alan lived close to the rescue site and agreed to meet us there with a hacksaw and various cutters. He brought with him John Hicks, one of the founding members of International Animal Rescue who happened to be over from India staying with Alan at the time.

The dog walker met us at the woodland car park and led us to the deer. It was at least a mile's walk into the forest. Having arrived at the spot where he'd first witnessed the head-locked deer, they were nowhere to be seen. We hunted around for a while and eventually spotted them further into the woodland. One of the deer was on the ground and had clearly died, but the other was standing with its head down, attached to the antlers of the other deer. As we approached the deer slipped down into a stream, clearly very exhausted. With Alan and John on one side of the stream , I approached from the other with one of our new volunteers.

Till now most of the deer I had dealt with were road casualties or caught in fencing and gates. So when a deer is mobile how do you catch it? Well, it's a good job I did rugby at college! I chose my moment and as the deer slipped down into the stream onto his knees, I launched myself across the stream and tackled the deer using my full body weight to pin him to the floor. I didn't really think about it, and never having tackled a deer before, I just flung myself at it hoping against hope that I wasn't doing more harm than good. This tactic seemed to work and we managed to pin him down.

We could then see what had happened; the two sets of antlers were attached to each other by bailer twine. It was likely that one of the deer already had the discarded twine attached to its antlers, having picked it up while grazing or going through a hedgerow. The pair had then engaged in rutting, where two males go for each other with head-on collisions. As a result, the second deer had also become entangled in the twine and joined to the first one. The deer that had died had probably done so because of the stress caused by being attached to and dragged round by the stronger deer. But even the surviving deer was in a bad way, very distressed, panicking and wanting to get free.

Kneeling in the mud and water of the stream, we set about cutting the twine in order to free the deer.   Before releasing him, I quickly checked over his head and neck to ensure there were no injuries, and after telling everyone to stand back, I jumped away clear of the deer and to safety. I sat there with my feet in the muddy water and watched as the deer sprang to life.   Such rescues are quite an emotional rollercoaster. One minute your heart is pounding away and you are feeling extremely stressed and anxious trying to catch and secure the animal safely, worried about what would happen if it escapes. The next minute you're breathing a sigh of relief, elated that the creature you have tried to help is safe and free.

Autumn 2004 saw a number of unusual rescue calls including a badger at Grove Hill near Hellingly, which had somehow managed to get itself caught inside a rabbit trap. It was not easy to release as the sizeable badger took up so much space in the rabbit-sized trap. Thought to be a troublesome teenager, the badger was probably being adventurous. We had to use screwdrivers in order to reach in, without being bitten, unlock the trap and free the trigger mechanism that was holding the door shut. As the trap and its ensnared badger were well away from any busy roads we decided to release the badger there and then, rather than bring him in for the rest of the day. Having managed to operate the unlocking mechanism, the badger was free. He quickly ran off across the field back to his home, where I like to imagine that he received a bit of a wigging from his worried parents. Teenagers will be teenagers, be they boy or badger.

Another unusual rescue was a call-out to Sovereign Harbour, Eastbourne. A dolphin had been spotted swimming around directly in front of the lock gates. Staff at Sovereign Harbour called me and asked if we would go over and check to see if it was ok. Wearing my British Divers Marine Life Rescue hat, I observed and monitored the dolphin. At first several members of the public claimed it was not well. After watching its behaviour from the harbour wall we decided to take a boat out and see how it reacted. We couldn't get anywhere near it - which is a good sign. We returned to the harbour wall to continue our observations and it soon became clear the dolphin was catching fish. After a few hours a couple of fishing boats left through the lock gates and the dolphin, possibly spotting its chance, disappeared with them out to sea.

A few days later, at 2am, I was awoken by a call from a lady in Peacehaven. She had a bat in her boudoir. She was quite frightened and would not go back into her bedroom. So, in the early hours of the morning, I drove to Peacehaven but when I opened her bedroom door there was no sign of any bat. The window was open and it was possible the bat had escaped, but I agreed to check round and make sure. As the lady had canvas wardrobes, an appealing hidey-hole for a bat to crawl into, there was a lot of checking to be done. Eventually I found the bat hiding down the side of the wardrobe and it was fairly easy to catch. Wearing gloves, I checked him over and noticed he was rather underweight, so instead of releasing him the following morning I took him to Jenny Clark who runs the Sussex Bat Hospital from her home in Forest Row. She identified the bat as a serotine, one of Britain's largest bats. Luckily I had been trained by Jenny in bat rescue and knew how to hold and handle them safely. After a few days of feeding up he was returned to Peacehaven and released.

Now I'm not the best of people at dealing with things at height. I don't mind wearing ropes and harnesses, but I'd rather not stand at the edge of a cliff for example. So I wasn't overly keen on attending a rescue on the old Hastings Pier. A rather confused female fox had managed to get onto the pier and worryingly had fallen asleep right on the edge of it, with a huge drop next to her. When I arrived it was clear the fox was not well and in need of some help. My concern was that in our attempt to catch her, she would fall into the water. I realised, with a certain degree of dismay, that the rescue attempt would involve me having to climb over the edge of the safety railings. We put a call into the local lifeboat station and asked if they had an inshore boat available which could provide me with a certain degree of safety. As it happened a boat was already out and about in the area, so they arrived quickly at the pier, and stood by just in case.

It turned out that the fox was far livelier than expected and gave me quite a run around, before I eventually managed to corner and catch her. We took her to one of our outdoor pens at Hailsham where she was given medication and allowed to recuperate.

Possibly the most amusing rescue of 2004 happened late in the evening at Normans Bay. We received a call about a deer with baler twine attached to its antlers and caught up on a branch in a hedgerow. I was concerned about the location. The deer was right at the top of a steep embankment at the end of a drainage dyke. If the deer slipped, the twine could easily have strangled it. I phoned fellow rescuers Val and Murrae Hume to come over and assist me, but while they were on their way, the deer started to thrash about and in the dark I was worried it could end up in the ice-covered dyke. Suddenly the deer broke free from the hedgerow and rushed straight towards me. He crashed into me, sent me flying backwards and bottom-first into the icy dyke. I emerged from the freezing water unhurt, but soaked from head to toe and covered in mud. Unfortunately the deer still had the twine wrapped round its antlers, but it was now going to be impossible to catch it. I cancelled the incoming support, slightly relieved that they hadn't arrived in time to see my ignominious dunking, and dripped and shivered my way back to my ambulance and drove up the road to the emergency vet clinic. While the staff there were used to seeing me arrive with bedraggled wildlife in need of help, it was the first time they had encountered a mud-covered human requiring a bit of their TLC. They provided me with a much welcome hot cup of coffee to warm my insides, and a heater and some towels to dry off and revitalize up my shivering exterior. I was absolutely frozen, but I did manage to laugh and see the funny side of it. As, it has to be said, did the surprised vets.

Just as the year had started, with loads of dead pigeons scattered along a road at Telscombe, it came to an end with a huge pile of dead rabbits dumped at the side of the A26 between Newhaven and Lewes. There were over fifty wild rabbits in total. I picked up a couple and took them to a local vet to establish the cause of death. His conclusion was that they had been shot. We reported the incident to Lewes District Council who cleared them away. The surrounding farm land was used for grazing rather than for crops, and to this day I really can't imagine why someone would bother shooting all those rabbits, and then just dumping them. Like the massacred pigeons, were these rabbits shot just for fun? If so, there must be people out there with a very warped sense of humour.

Chapter 11 - The Devil and the Deep Blue Sea.

By the early 2000s our rescue work had grown to the point where it was necessary for us to become a registered charity. Otherwise we could not apply for grants or be eligible for sponsorship. I spoke to a number of people already running charities who warned me of the hassle, paperwork and red tape which came with it. It was also unclear which type of charity we should set up. Over the years I had made several attempts at building up a committee and trying to organise WRAS in a better way. Many people came and went, some were a god send and others just wanted to tell everyone what they should be doing and not actually do anything themselves. In 2003 and into 2005 we were lucky to have Jill join us as a volunteer. As well as the practical side of things she was an excellent administrator. She was great at researching and compiling the necessary paperwork, getting advice and dealing with the bureaucracy. Together with Murrae, Val, Peter, Sue, Julia, Kevin and Paula, we had our first proper committee and WRAS became a registered charitable company early 2005.

I am sure you have heard of the Berlin Wall but have you heard of the Westham Wall? In the spring of 2005 I was called to Westham Pond at Peelings Lane after a dispute broke out between the locals. I don't mean people but waterfowl! A pair of Canada Geese had nested on the island and hatched several goslings. However a pair of swans had flown in and decided to take over the nest and lay their eggs.

Some local residents contacted us after seeing the swans chasing off the geese and having a go at their goslings. In a natural environment in the countryside, the swans would probably have nested elsewhere without a problem. However on park ponds disputes like this occur because of the artificial feeding administered by humans, and neither family wanting to leave because of the easy supply of food.

After lengthy discussions with the Swan Sanctuary and the local parish council, it was decided we should erect the Westham Wall. Using a role of orange safety mesh, the sort you see at building sites to cordon off separate areas, we put up a barrier across the pond and up its respective banks. The idea was to keep the Canada Geese on one side and the swans on the other.

The geese were more than happy but the cob swan wasn't best pleased. He would patrol up and down the barrier staring malevolently at the geese whilst his partner sat on the nest happily incubating her eggs.

Everything seemed to work well, apart from a couple of occasions when the cob swan decided to walk up onto the pavement and round the barrier, leading to a barrage of calls from concerned local residents as the cob started attacking the geese chasing them up onto the road.

But the problems started big time when the cygnets hatched. Dad was not impressed with having to share the pond. He kept challenging the barrier and almost flying into it. He became much more aggressive as a result. Eventually he did fly into the barrier knocking it down and having a go at the geese again. The cob swan was very territorial and seemed to get very frustrated that the geese were present. Residents called us down to the pond after the cob flattened the fence. We re-erected it but within minutes he was attempting another assault trying to get through. The geese were becoming more distressed as were local residents who continued to bombard us with calls.

We contacted the Wildlife Officer at Sussex Police and a wildlife advisor at Natural England. We told them about the Westham Wall and how we had done our best to resolve the situation without moving the geese. They agreed that we would now be within our rights to catch and rescue them. The Canada Geese were found a safe home at a sanctuary, and both goslings and cygnets grew up to be healthy, happy and strong.

We did receive some criticism that we should have stepped in sooner; "Why didn't you take them away at the start". Helping wildlife is not about taking the easiest option, nor about jumping to conclusions about what might happen. Taking any wildlife away from its natural habitat should always be done as a last resort. We wouldn't want to be taken away or forced to move from our homes. Well neither does our wildlife! It can also cause them unnecessary stress. The Westham Wall has now fallen!

The next few years proved to be very difficult for me. Apart from being diagnosed as having extremely high blood pressure, I started suffering from what I can only describe as a sensation of falling and vertigo. Several times I actually fell over, and on a few occasions I found myself waking up at night having to hold onto the bed tightly feeling as though I was falling and becoming very disorientated and sick.

It was very frightening, and the more it happened, the more worrying it became. I tried my best to carry on with my rescue work which, during the busy season, was frequently some fifteen to twenty hours a day, with very little time off.

I had been appointed the National Co-ordinator for British Divers Marine Life Rescue (BDMLR) at Uckfield. I was working three days week for them but spent most of the week at their office, trying to balance my time and energy between WRAS and BDMLR.

I was living part time in Seaford with my girlfriend, Sue, who joined me at BDMLR.

I met Sue via a rescue call to an injured gull in front of her flat. She is the best advertisement for a vegan diet anyone could need. She looked fantastic, was fit and healthy and everyone used to comment on how young she looked and couldn't believe her age. I was neither very clear about what a vegan was nor understood what it involved before I met her. But whatever it was, I felt it might do me some good were I to adopt it too. Sue explained that veganism is similar to a vegetarian diet and excludes meat, eggs, honey, dairy products and all other animal-derived ingredients. Many vegans also do not eat foods that are processed using animal products, such as refined white sugar and some wines.

Ever since I have tried to avoid dairy products and where possible use vegan options if available, but I admit I do find it difficult with my hectic lifestyle. I've never been one to force vegetarianism or veganism on anyone. It has to be their choice. There is no point doing it as a fad or the latest craze. I still have an allergy to milk so I've not drunk it for years apart from in small quantities in cooking. The first soya milks which were available in the 1970s and 80s were disgusting, and really put me off drinking anything like it. It was not till I met Sue that I tried Alpro soya milk and loved it. I could finally have milk shakes again!

In December 2005 Murrae, Alec and myself as well as fellow BDMLR medic Kevin, did a ten day round trip to Scotland. Its purpose was to learn as much as we could about seals; how to handle, rescue and care for them. The Scottish waters abound in grey seals and the coast dotted with seal hospitals, including one run by the BDMLR, so it was the perfect place to hone our seal rescue skills.

First stop was a small seal hospital in the Sealife Centre in Oban. This was managed by Jamie and Heather who taught us how to catch, handle and tube feed them safely. Next to Ullapool and another seal hospital, and then right up to the northern tip of Scotland, to Thurso near John O'Groats, where the seals we learnt to handle were much livelier.

We rounded off our trip in Montrose and finally down to Scarborough feeling far more confident about our ability to deal with seals as and when they eventuality should arise.

Although we don't get many grey seals off the coast of Sussex, we do have the smaller, common seals, and all the training in Scotland was invaluable when it came to catching, handling and treating these animals.

The next rescue didn't involve a seal, but a most unusual fox rescue. The call came from a mobile phone shop in George Street, Hove. When the staff had opened the shop first thing in the morning they were surprised to find a fox's leg hanging down from the ceiling through a hole where a light should be. They deducted, correctly, that the rest of the fox was attached to the leg and stuck in the ceiling cavity.

Rescuer Maz, who lived in Brighton, came to help out with the rescue. We were shown upstairs to a disused and dilapidated flat. It was clear the foxes were living there as the rear door was off its hinges and there was fox poo everywhere. Several floor boards were missing and the foxes had been able to get underneath and use the ceiling space as a den.

It took us a while to find the fox, which had now moved. We tried removing some more floor boards but quickly realised that we couldn't reach the fox from above due to a layer of asbestos. Our only way to reach the fox would be from below - from the mobile phone shop. This was not the news the shop owners wanted to hear.

The shop shut for business while we removed several ceiling tiles and knocked holes in the plastered ceiling above. Armed with a torch, I stuck my heard through one of the holes and spotted the fox over in a corner. We took out yet more ceiling tiles and plaster and three hours later, by means of a dog grasper, I finally managed to catch the fox and place it into a waiting cage.

We took the fox to our new holding unit at the back of a vet's in Hailsham where it could rest and be treated for a minor form of mange.

That was quite enough fox-foraging for one day, or so I thought. The very next morning we had another call about a trapped fox. This one had chosen a disused car show room in Kemptown, Brighton. By chance we had a Meridian TV crew following us for the day. They came with us to film the rescue.

We were shown where the fox had been living, and systematically started working our way through the building trying to find it. The reason we needed to catch the fox was because the building was about to be demolished and the last thing the workers wanted was for the fox to get killed in the process. We hunted high and low but to no avail. With a sense of déjà vu, I realised there was only one place remaining where the fox could be - in the suspended ceiling cavity of the showroom. But at least this building was about to be pulled down and didn't have distraught shop assistants anxiously watching as their showroom was dismantled, ceiling tile by ceiling tile.

We started knocking out the roof tiles one by one, gradually reducing the area in which the fox could travel. At the start of each section of roof we would remove a tile and using a torch check to see if the fox was present. All of a sudden the fox appeared, walking along a steel joist at the edge of the ceiling. I ran and grabbed the dog grasper but was too late, the fox disappeared. Off we set again, searching all the rooms for wily Mr Fox. Some ten minutes later we found it. It had jumped down from its ceiling hide-out and had run into one of the offices. Here we were able to corner him, get a towel over his head and secure the frightened animal. We took the fox to join the other at our holding centre, hoping our foxy escapades were over. However the vulpine fun and games didn't end there. A call came in – from the mobile phone shop in Hove. They had another fox in their roof! We drove back to Hove and started the whole process all over again. At least we knew it was not the same fox from the day before, as that one was still at our centre.

This time the fox had managed to get itself wedged under the flat roof of the extension at the rear of the shop. We cut two holes in the ceiling and, pushing with a broom from one end and dog grasper from the other, we managed to encourage the fox towards a suitable hole where we could get it out. Using a towel and gauntlet gloves to protect myself I reached in, grabbed the fox by the scruff of its neck and brought it down to a waiting cage. It might sound quick, but the whole process from start to finish took over four hours and we were sweating buckets due to the heat in the ceiling space.

A hot four hour fox rescue is one thing, but dealing with a bureaucratic job's worth is quite another, and I know which I prefer any day. When they happen simultaneously it's enough to try the patience of a saint, which I am not.

Whilst we were attempting to rescue the mobile phone shop fox, the local parking wardens came knocking on the door asking us to remove our ambulances from the street. We explained we were doing a rescue and even invited them in so they could see for themselves. But to no avail, they demanded we moved them. We refused, saying that if the police or fire service were here then they would not be expected to move their vehicles. About an hour later the wardens returned with a supervisor and threatened to tow our vehicles away. So we said please do, because it will be filmed by Meridian TV, who were still with us, and we would also be contacting the local press. Just as we were finishing the rescue and taking the caged fox to our ambulance, a tow truck arrived. We put the fox in the ambulance, stood back and waited to see what they would do. A team of four parking wardens were standing down the street watching from a distance. The tow-truck driver jumped down from his lorry and said he had been asked to remove the ambulance from the street. We explained the situation to him and, with Meridian TV filming the entire event, the driver said, "I don't get paid enough to put up with this!" With which he climbed back into his lorry and drove off. Following his lead, we boarded our ambulance and headed away. As we passed the disgruntled row of parking wardens we waved them a cheery goodbye.

In 2005 Bird Flu was at its height. Everyone was panicking and phoning up all the time because they had seen a dead bird and were worried about whether or not they would catch bird flu. We decided to try and do something which might help. Working with F10, a veterinary disinfectant company, we decided to give away 500 bottles of disinfectant.

Although not a cure for Bird Flu, the disinfectant destroys the virus which causes it. We asked people to ensure their bird tables were clean and hygienic by washing and cleaning them at least once a week with this disinfectant. This would help fight bird flu and help prevent it spreading via bird tables in our area.

My sleep levels were really taking a battering that year and the amount of work I was doing for WRAS and BDMLR was starting to take its toll. My doctor sent me for an MRI scan at Hurstwood Park Neurological Unit at Haywards Heath. Luckily the scan did not show anything horrible. I described the dizzy spells and sense of falling to the consultant and he explained that this was an unusual type of migraine. He said there was likely to be a trigger and it would be a process of elimination to discover what that trigger was.

Over the next 12 months, suffering numerous dizzy spells, and trying different tablets to attempt to control my blood pressure, I discovered a pattern. I seemed to suffer from these migraines about three days after occasions when I had been working through the night without any sleep. I think this was my body telling me I needed to be careful and not over-stretch myself, and I hadn't been listening to it.

Eventually my blood pressure rocketed sky high. One night I had a migraine and the doctor came very close to admitting me to hospital but instead decided to sedate me in order to bring my blood pressure down. The following day he gave me a severe telling off and told me I must take some time off work. Meekly I agreed, and Maz, Murrae and Alec kindly took over the rescue phone for a few days to give me a break.

I had been given a serious warning that if I did not start taking it easy I was likely to have a heart attack. With our new holding facility in Hailsham I needed to find someone to take on some of my responsibilities. I was very limited in my options, but I had recently been working with someone from a neighbouring rescue set-up who had good assessment skills and suitable experience so I invited him to take over some of my work; looking after and treating the casualties in our care.

Sadly this decision proved to be a big, though unforeseeable, mistake. After a few months I discovered he had become homeless and was sleeping in his car. I offered him my sofa for a few nights whilst he sorted himself out. Not only did a few nights turn into four months, but unfortunately he turned out to be a somewhat unreliable helper. He managed to run up huge veterinary bills which almost ran WRAS into the ground. He also played people off against each other which caused a great deal of upset and damage to our fledgling charity.

A number of people blamed me for the problems, but whenever I asked anyone to come up with a solution, they couldn't.   The whole situation became very stressful to the point that it ruined the relationship with my girlfriend. I was trying so hard to keep a balance between my health, WRAS's workload, my girlfriend and being able to earn a living to pay the bills and to eat.

The situation looked bleak. WRAS was on the point of bankruptcy through over-spending and not knowing when to say "no" for the sake of the animals already in care.

I was almost in despair when help came from a rather unexpected source. My father had recently sold our family home. From the proceeds he generously gave my brother and I a small cheque. I was able to put £10,000, a large portion of my share, into WRAS to keep it going. This proved to be a life-saver, and one for which I am eternally grateful.

Chapter 12. I'm not sure which is worse, people or animals!

Many people may remember the Thames whale rescue in January 2006. What most won't have been aware of was a second rescue that was taking place at the same time up in Cumbria. As the National Co-ordinator for British Divers Marine Life Rescue, I was sent to the small town of Maryport on the Cumbrian coast. The Whale and Dolphin Conservation Society (WDCS) had been called out as well.

A young male bottlenose dolphin was trapped inside one of the town's two marinas. It had apparently been there for well over a week and was starting to attract regular visitors to the town to dolphin-watch.

The Harbour Office asked us what could be done to resolve the problem. Our first job was to assess the dolphin's condition, to monitor its behaviour and establish whether it was trapped or not.

Some of the local residents claimed they had seen it swimming freely in and out through the lock gates and that it wasn't trapped at all.

Along with Laura, from WDCS , we spent four days providing a round the clock watch on the dolphin to find out whether it was inside or outside the harbour. Not once did we see it outside. We also took photos of the dolphin's body condition, primarily checking its lumbar muscle which should be convex if healthy. The photos showed the muscle to be in a reasonable condition.

About a week into our stay we began to get concerned; the weather was growing colder and ice was starting to form at one end of the marina. The water in the marina is brackish, which means it is partially salt and partially fresh water. Dolphins can survive in fresh water but long term it is not good for them.

As far as food went, there were quite a few fish in the harbour and it was obvious that the dolphin was catching fish when we first visited.

After consulting the directors at BDMLR and discussions with WDCS, it was decided that the best course of action would be to try and push the dolphin out of the brackish waters of the marina and into the salty sea. Alan Knight, accompanied by head vet James and other local Marine Mammal Medics, using several boats and a pinner, (a device with repeatedly emits a noise and is designed to work in water) attempted to push the dolphin out. It didn't want to go.

We then looked at how dolphins had been encouraged out of harbours not only in other parts of the UK but also across the world. We tried encouraging the dolphin out of the harbour by trying to get the young dolphin to play with a buoy using buoys attached to boats, but every time it got close to the lock gates it turned and refused to leave. After a few hours of trying it was decided this was not going to work.

The next plan was to enlist the help of Doug, a former dolphin trainer now turned campaigner. Laura and I were given the job of working with him. Doug had various thoughts on how we might lure the dolphin out of the marina.

We tried encouraging him to follow floating buoys, and we also left various items like balls floating on the water to see if he would play with them. But the dolphin just wasn't interested.

We then decided to try a home-made "bubble curtain", a device often used by dolphin aquariums to confine dolphins in tanks. The bubbles confuse the dolphins by interfering with their echo-location system, making them think that there is in fact an obstruction which they won't cross. We managed to acquire an air compressor from a local company as well as some old hoses in which we drilled numerous holes. Rob and Jenny, BDMLR's Cumbrian Co-ordinators, then donned their diving equipment and swam down to lay the hoses on the bed of the marina in an arc from one side of the lock entrance to the other. We tested this several times and after a few adjustments the hoses seemed to work fairly well, and when attached to the air compressor sent up a curtain of bubbles.

We then waited and watched the dolphin to see if it would cross the line of the air hose, and every time it did we turned on the bubble air curtain. It was hoped that this would give the dolphin no choice but to leave the harbour as it would not want to retreat back over the bubbles.

To our frustration every time we fired up the air compressor, the dolphin challenged the curtain of bubbles it created, and promptly swam back through them and into the marina. This came as a real surprise. We were now completely perplexed as to why it didn't seem to want to leave?

That evening we sat down and started trying to figure out what on earth might be stopping the dolphin from leaving. Was it a young solitary dolphin enjoying the attention it was getting from the locals? Was it staying because a local fisherman kept dumping fish in the marina for it to eat? Was it confused by the construction of the lock gate? This last suggestion began to ring bells.

One of us remembered having read details about an incident in an open harbour where a stranded dolphin had been re-floated but could not find its way out to sea. It was thought that the dolphin's echolocation was misleading the dolphin into thinking it was trapped, enclosed by the harbour wall. What the dolphin hadn't realised, and what his normally sophisticated and highly tuned echolocation system hadn't indicated, was that there was a right hand turn to get out. At Maryport, the marina was at right angles to the river entrance, and on the opposite side of the river was a harbour wall, so at high tide the echolocation would bounce off the wall and, to the dolphin, would appear as a dead end corridor.

We believed that this had to be the reason our young bottlenose wouldn't leave the harbour, so what was the solution? We started considering other means of releasing him, or whether capture would be possible.

I suggested leaving the lock gates open and letting the water drain out gradually and naturally as the tide receded. Initially this idea was dismissed as various people mistakenly thought I was talking about opening the lock gate and letting the water flood out rapidly. Which I certainly wasn't !

But by now it had become apparent that we were running out of time. We had been there two weeks and the dolphin's condition was deteriorating. By comparing earlier photos with the most recent it was clear that the lumbar muscle was much reduced and the dolphin was losing body condition.

A rescue mission had to be affected if we were to stand any chance of saving the dolphin. We would have to physically remove him from the marina and place him into the open sea. This was not going to be an easy operation, but it was made even more difficult and frustrating by the attitude of some of the locals. Many of them were vehemently opposed to us removing the dolphin at all. He had become quite a tourist attraction, bringing visitors into the town at a time of year when it would normally be very quiet. Believe it nor not, we even received death threats from people who said our lives would not be worth living if we killed the dolphin. Some even accused us of wanting to remove it just to kill it. Who in their right mind would want to do that?

The rescue mission was planned with the help of one of our cetacean vets from Scotland and various experienced marine mammal medics from across the country. We all met at the coastguard station and meticulously plotted out the details. We knew it had to be quick and everything needed to be in place for the rescue to be a success.

At high tide the lock gates were opened and left open. As the tide went out the water level in the harbour slowly sank. The local fire service, coastguard and police were on site as back-up in case of problems with the mud. We moved a large floating pontoon across the lock gates to prevent the dolphin from injuring himself as the water drained out. A boat was used to ensure the dolphin ended up in the middle of the last open section of water.

Four Medics in dry suits waded out across one side of the remaining pool of water with a large cargo type net, weighted along one edge. They slowly dragged the net across the pool and Doug went inside the netted area to help with the capture. He waited until the dolphin challenged the net and then, amidst a great deal of splashing, he and the four medics had to secure the dolphin. They then had to lift the dolphin to the surface of the water as quickly as possible to prevent it going into a dive reflex and potentially drowning.

They then moved the dolphin towards the waiting boat and stretcher. At this point I jumped into the water to help hold the dolphin and get the stretcher underneath him and secured.

A huge crane was waiting on the harbour side to lift the stretcher out of the water. Whilst Alan and the medics were securing the stretcher to the crane, I scrambled up a vertical ladder to the top of the harbour wall and onto the inshore rescue boat which was on a trailer ready and waiting to do a beach launch. A scoop stretcher was placed across the front of the rescue boat and lined with a semi-inflated air bed. Cameron the Vet was already on the boat to check the

dolphin over. We stood by as the dolphin was gently hoisted up to street level and down onto the rescue boat by the crane. As soon as it was detached from the crane a tractor, usually used by the RNLI to launch their rescue boat, pulled the trailer with its precious cargo down the short distance to the beach. Whilst traveling this short distance a group of people on the bank started shouting "Murderers!"

Within minutes the boat was in the water and out to sea. It took only a few more minutes to get 8 metres of water beneath us and, ensuring we were away from any nets, the dolphin was then gently tipped over the edge of the boat and back into the water where it swam away. To our surprise a second dolphin appeared and they both breached the water several times before disappearing out to sea. From the start to finish the whole process of rescue and release took just 15-20minutes. We were all delighted and celebrated that night in a local pub.

To our amazement and dismay, in the local paper the following week we were accused of taking the dolphin out and shooting it because nobody had managed to get any video footage of the release. I am really not sure what part of Wildlife Rescue and Marine Life Rescue people don't understand - we want to save wildlife not kill it! I would have thought the word "rescue" might have been a clue.

Sadly the problems at Maryport didn't end there. A few months later a couple of dolphins were spotted playing with boats just off-shore. We later found out that a small boat had originally tempted the bottlenose dolphin into the harbour using fish as bait.

Over the following couple of years we had more and more problems and reports of people trying to interact with this dolphin which the locals named "Marra" which locally means "friend."

More and more people started interacting with the dolphin which we now classed as a Solitary Social Dolphin - one which does not belong to a social pod, craves company and starts to interact with people. Normally such solitary dolphins would meet up with other solitary dolphins and form a new pod but their numbers are so low it is difficult for them to find other solitary dolphins.

Sadly despite warnings asking people to keep their distance and respect "Marra" for being wild many people ignored this and more and more people started trying to swim with him. A short distance down the coast, a local family went out swimming with the dolphin but had to leave the water because he started to play rather too roughly with them for their liking. He started fixating on women and would try and isolate them. On one occasion he back flipped and his tail landed straight on a lady's head. He also started charging at people in the water getting very rough. This started frightening the swimmers to the point that they had to leave the water. But dolphins will be dolphins; they are powerful, they are wild, they love playing and just don't know their own strength. They will also think that humans who want to swim and play with them are just another kind of dolphin, and are up for the rough and tumble that dolphins enjoy.

There were also several occasions when Marra was found to have injuries to his dorsal fin and inevitably what we had warned people of and feared came true. Marra was eventually found washed up dead on a local beach with injuries that most likely had caused his death.

It is occasions like this that make you realise how selfish humans can be; they can't see the bigger picture and how dangerous their actions can be. Some people seem to think that their one little action won't make a difference, but unfortunately it is the repeated actions of the many which will. Selfishness is all too common an issue when dealing with the interactions between wildlife and people.

Later that year, while still working for BDMLR, but back in Sussex, we received a call from Skegness about two whales beached on the shore. We were told the site was at least a mile from the town of Skegness and access was extremely difficult. BDMLR have whale rescue pontoons strategically positioned around the country. There was one set in Lincoln but the problem was that these were Northern Bottlenose Whales; they require two sets of pontoons each so we arranged sets from Newcastle and Liverpool to be driven down. The next nearest sets were in Kent and at our office in Uckfield. These we decided to load into a vehicle and then made a few phone calls. Following the famous Thames Whale rescue several people had offered the use of helicopters and planes. Someone at Rochester Airport put out a message for us requesting help, and a person with a helicopter responded. We drove the equipment up to the airport where Alan Knight and I met up with three other medics to await the arrival of the promised helicopter. We were all somewhat surprised and stunned to see a Harrods Department Store Westland AW Grand Lux Helicopter touchdown. Surely not for us? But it was! I had never flown in any kind of aircraft before and was rather nervous. I had taken the precaution of having travel sickness tablets with me. We loaded the equipment on board and sat in the rather posh rear cabin. I was not brilliant with heights and sat as still as I could with my eyes focused firmly forwards. As the helicopter started it was a very strange and rather unnerving feeling. When we took off it was like sitting on top of a moving washing machine on a spin cycle. After about 20minutes I plucked up the courage to look out of the window and down at the vista below. To my surprise I felt ok. I soon got used to the flight and enjoyed the unaccustomed birds-eye view. Within 45 minutes of leaving Rochester we were landing on the sandy beach at Skegness and unloading the equipment, thanks to the coastguard who had guided us in using smoke flares.

One of the beached whales was already dead but the other was very much alive although not in a brilliant condition. I had my reservations about the whale being re-floated but those in charge decided to give it a try. The rescue was not without risk and by the time high tide arrived it was dark and we were working by torchlight. Despite a valiant effort by a huge team of BDMLR medics the whale was found washed up dead at first light.

After a series of frustrating Northern Bottlenose Whale rescues a meeting with the Marine Animal Rescue Coalition was organised; this included the Whale and Dolphin Conservation Society, Zoological Society of London (ZSL), BDMLR, RSPCA and others. The ZSL gave a presentation on the findings of all the recent Northern Bottlenose Whale incidents looking at similarities between the strandings. The resulting prognosis was that this particular type of deep diving whale struggles with muscle myopathy and the cause of death is from the weight of the animal's body crushing its internal organs when stranded on the hard surface of a beach.

Despite trying to take it easy, 2007 was still a busy year and proved to be a lot of work. The outbreak of foot and mouth disease was a big blow and caused a lot of problems. Trying to get updates out of officials at DEFRA was like trying to get blood out of a stone. Someone would tell you one thing, the next minute somebody would tell you something completely different.

I was in the middle of dealing with a road casualty deer and liaising with St Tiggywinkles for its rehabilitation when I heard about the imposition of movement restrictions. I realised that the deer would have to be isolated so as not to come into contact with any other animals. Under normal circumstances, we would have taken her straight to the specialist deer unit at St Tiggywinkles in Buckinghamshire, but this would have meant crossing county boundaries. So instead we took her to the Sussex Horse Rescue Sanctuary in nearby Uckfield. Here she was bedded down in an isolated stable and we called a vet to examine her and help with her care.

She was the last injured or sick deer we were able to take in and care for while the movement restrictions were in place. The same applied to hedgehogs and apart from them no other wildlife was affected.

This meant that where normally we would have gone out and picked up a hedgehog and brought it back to the centre for care, we were now not allowed to. They had to be left where they were found. Several times we obtained medication from vets so that hedgehogs could be treated on site, but it was very unsatisfactory and as a result there is no doubt that animals suffered.

To me it seemed hypocritical that in order to prevent financial loss to the meat industry, wildlife ended up having to suffer. There were a few occasions when, unable to move casualties to the vets, we would call the vet to come to them to euthanize those that were clearly too sick or injured to survive.

In other instances we handed out carriers and helped support people who were looking after poorly hedgehogs in their garden sheds. It was far from satisfactory and very frustrating.

Unfortunately one of the drawbacks of WRAS getting bigger and being more in the public eye was that many more people were watching what we were doing. We found ourselves under the public microscope and had to be much more careful about what we do. There are some smaller organisations and individuals who tell us we should ignore the law, but for the sake of the thousands of animals we deal with I can't afford to risk a jealous or anti-wildlife person reporting us, as it would put the whole future of our work at risk.

So I stuck to the rules, frustrating and upsetting as it was at times.

Treating minor injuries on site was ok, but dealing with more serious injuries was very difficult and some animals ended up having to be euthanized in order to prevent them suffering, especially in cases where the finders were not willing or happy to help look after the hedgehog. I lost my temper on several occasion with DEFRA trying to get accurate information, no one seemed to know what was happening and the correct procedures. I can understand why they put movement restrictions in place for cattle and other farmed animals, but not for injured wildlife. If bio security is undertaken then I really can't see how we would be causing a problem.

Later that year I was horrified when one of our volunteers phoned to say that approximately £2,000 worth of outdoor metal cages had been stolen from a site we had use of in Lower Dicker. The purpose built pens were only a year old, and were used during the busy spring and early summer periods to rehabilitate injured and orphaned birds.

The cages had not been in use for a few months over the winter, and the owner of the site told me that they had disappeared sometime during November and December and he had assumed that we had taken them away. Unfortunately this was not the case and the theft was not discovered till my colleague Alec arrived to check and prepare them for use in spring.

What annoyed me most of all was that these pens had been paid for by kind donations from members of the public and from our volunteers' hard work fundraising.

The incident was reported to the Police but as they had disappeared several months previously, it was unlikely that we would ever get them back.

Having valuable cages stolen is one thing, they can be replaced, but losing a valued and entertaining volunteer is quite another.

Summer 2008 saw rescuer Maz having to retire due to severe arthritis. Maz was a character, and drove one of our ambulances based in Hove. He was on call for most of the week, going out on rescues whenever and as often as he could. He also helped me out big time by taking the phone whilst I was at work and occasionally over-night. He would describe himself as a vegan, hippy, anarchist, atheist, dyslexic and a staunch animal rights campaigner. If there was anything

happening locally to raise awareness of animal cruelty or abuse, he would be there; be it demonstrating outside the Sea Life Centre at Brighton, or helping to rescue hundreds of emaciated Yorkshire terriers found in some garden sheds at Burgess Hill, Maz would be on hand getting his hands dirty and putting the animals first. He was a laugh to work with and we did some great rescues together.

Maz was due to get his rabies injections and attend a bat handling course. But just a few days before this, we had a call-out to a bat in Brighton. I made it absolutely clear to him saying "Whatever you do, wear gloves and don't get bitten!" When he arrived the finder had the bat in his bare hands and passed it to Maz who also wasn't wearing gloves. The inevitable happened and Maz promptly got bitten! Even more unfortunately the bat turned out to be one of the species that can carry rabies. So after boxing up the bat, I told him to go straight to the hospital as he would need a rabies injection.

The bat was taken to Sheila at the Sussex Bat Group and Maz headed to Brighton Hospital A&E department. He told the doctor what had happened but the doctor dismissed the need for any treatment. However Maz wasn't to be turned away that easily and he pushed them to check what the procedure was for a bat bite. The doctor duly went off to check, and was away for what seemed like ages. He suddenly re-appeared, somewhat panicked and unsure what to do. He said that a courier was bringing some injections down to the hospital and that Maz would get seen as soon as possible. He then proceeded to fill out large amounts of paperwork.

Maz ended up having various injections as a precaution and suffered nothing worse than a bruised arm - and a bruised ego. We weren't going to let him live that one down in a hurry! The rescued bat, however, was now on death row.

Such incidents have to be reported to DEFRA. They doubtless filled out yet more paperwork and issued a destruction notice for the bat without even seeing it, never mind assessing it for rabies. Both WRAS and the Sussex Bat Group leapt to the bat's defence, refusing to release it for destruction. DEFRA officials, and indeed the police, then paid a visit to Sheila and the bat. Sheila stood her ground. She said that the bat was showing no signs of rabies; it had only bitten Maz because it was a rescue situation and the bat was frightened - not rabid mad. There was no need to destroy it!

When the guidelines for dealing with bat bites were written, they were designed for members of the public. Bats don't go round biting people as a matter of course, but are more likely to do so if they have rabies. So the protocols at the time assumed that if a bat bites it must be a rogue bat, and is likely to carry rabies. The guidelines don't take into consideration rescue situations where an animal could be injured or sick and bite as a result of discomfort, fear or fright but not necessarily have rabies. The bat was quarantined and monitored and showed no signs of illness, and eventually DEFRA gave in and lifted the order to destroy it. The bat was free to fly again, but Maz won't forget the trouble he caused that day!

In August 2008, I was asked to go down to Hayling Island after a Northern Bottlenose Whale was found swimming round in the shallow water of Chichester Harbour. We arrived at first light and in the pallid light of dawn we searched the area and found the whale had stranded overnight on mud flats.

We worked with Hampshire Fire Service to reach the whale. High pressure hoses were used to try to liquidise the mud in an attempt to get the whale back to water, but this failed as the whale was just too big and there was no way of getting lifting equipment close enough.

Such deep diving whales do not do well when they strand, and our six hour window to get him moved ran out. After talking to a national cetacean vet about our options, it was clear that euthanasia should be considered as the kindest and most realistic outcome. Unfortunately the vet and a number of medics on site were against this idea and completely ignored his advice.

As the tide came in the Fire Service and I decided it was too unsafe to stay with the whale but the volunteer medics refused to leave. At the last minute the local vet decided to try and euthanize the whale; an extremely unsafe thing to do on unstable mud flats, the tide coming in and a huge thrashing whale.

To avoid being injured by the distressed whale, they had no choice but to get to the nearby boats and leave the water. To my horror the vet and medics then used canoes to frighten the whale out to deeper water where it disappeared out of sight. A few hours later we received reports of the whale having stranded on a sand bank at the south western side of Hayling Island. By this time vets from the Zoological Society of London had arrived and taken over, swiftly euthanizing the whale.

When the dead whale was examined it turned out to be a very sick animal that clearly would not have survived re-flotation. Post mortem results also revealed extensive internal damage from being stranded on a hard surface for too long, demonstrating that euthanasia had been the kindest option all along.

I appreciate that people want to save wildlife, and after all I have dedicated my whole life to that end, but it's very important not to allow emotions to cloud one's judgement. There will always be occasions when euthanasia is the best outcome for the creature you are trying to prevent from suffering. It may not be what we humans want but it is often the best option for the casualty. It's not nice and it's not enjoyable, but at times it's by far the kindest thing to do.

In September 2008 we received a call to Eastbourne. The local paper had emailed us photos of strange looking objects seen on the Holywell Beach. The pictures showed misshapen lumpy mounds of pendulous tentacles and chalky black and white shells. We sent the pictures to Jamie Dyer, BDMLR's Scottish Co-ordinator (and former Sealife Manager), who identified them as Goose Barnacles. He'd seen them before.

Goose barnacles are extremely odd-looking crustaceans usually found in quite deep water. They have long fleshy necks (peduncles) with suckers on one end to anchor themselves, and on the other is a rather delicate chalky white heart-shaped shell with black stripy lines. Occasionally they can be found on debris that has become dislodged from the sea bed and washed up on the shore. They are found in oceans the world over, except in Arctic regions, and obviously the Eastbourne barnacles had been washed ashore in just such a fashion.

Jamie had seen massive congregations of goose barnacles where they attached themselves onto logs and other floating debris in the water, and then multiplied until the object is completely covered and unrecognisable. He had even had a turtle in from the Isle of Skye the previous year which had been covered by these long-necked crustaceans.

Jamie advised us that they looked fairly fresh still and viable so it was worth trying to get them back into the water, though there was a chance that they might just wash up again. Goose barnacles can only survive for a limited period of time out of water.

Rescuers Andy and Tony were sent down to the beach to assess whether the barnacles could be moved and returned to the sea, But when they got there they found that the tide had turned and had already re-floated them back to the salty waves. A strange rescue attempt, but at least I could now add goose barnacles to my ever growing list wildlife experiences.

In the warmer summer weather WRAS was visited by the television programme Animal 24:7. The presenter Tom Heap came over on several occasions and joined me on some rescues. One of the first calls was to Hastings. Two young badgers had fallen down an embankment into a garden and were unable to get out. When we arrived there was only one badger in the garden. It was clearly a youngster and just not big enough to climb up the embankment and away. We could see blood on the patio so decided it would be best to catch him and bring him in for a check-up. The badger was quite feisty and real character to deal with.

Later that day we also had a call to a fox cub trapped in a bin at the bottom of a garden. We watched and waited in a cold conservatory to see if the fox cub's mum would return and collect him. Sadly she didn't, so we took him back to the centre to be hand-reared.

After a long day rescuing we then had the job of trying to get the badger cub back to its home territory after dark. We managed to find a sett close to the Hastings garden where he was found, and after climbing the embankment we released the cub at the top and watched him run back to its home, probably to be told off by its mum for staying out all day!

On another visit from Tom Heap there were rescues a-plenty. A baby deer near Gatwick Airport which had to be assessed and then transported up to St Tiggywinkles; a gosling caught up in fishing line at Hampden Park; a rabbit stuck behind a radiator in Mayfield, and a road casualty and shot gull in Eastbourne. We also did a rescue with a difference when we were called to Newhaven after local residents were concerned about a family of swans in a drainage dyke next to the large supermarket. They were concerned that the two adult swans and cygnets could not get up the steep sides of the dyke. We drove over to take a look and decided not to rush in but stand back and observe. After a while the swans moved further up the dyke and managed to climb out and make their way over the grass and back to their main pond and nest. We then investigated what the swans had been doing and noticed that at the end of dyke there was an area covered in duck weed. This is a valuable source of food and nutrition for waterfowl. Unfortunately also in the dyke was a lot of polystyrene and litter, so out came WRAS's dry suits. I managed to persuade Tom to get down and dirty with me in the water to help clean out the rubbish to enable the swans and cygnets stay safe. I must say he did this with good grace and even a certain degree of enthusiasm. The resulting TV programme turned out to be very popular and a twist to the normal stories featured on the show.

The summer 2008 is when I met my girlfriend Kathy who had enquired about volunteering. If only she knew what she was letting herself in for! Kathy lived a stone's throw away up the lane from where I was now residing at the Sussex Horse Rescue Centre in Uckfield. The very first rescue I called her out to inadvertently sealed our relationship. I received a phone call about female fallow deer that had its leg caught up in electric fencing in a field at Blackboys. The caller had cut the deer free but it just sat there unable to get up. I phoned Kathy and asked her if she was available to help with the rescue. A few minutes later she met me in the lane and jumped on board the ambulance.

When we arrived the deer was still in the field on the ground. As we approached she tried to get up and run off but only managed to hobble to the edge of a small piece of woodland. She was obviously injured and in distress. I shouted across the field to Kathy to ask her to head the deer off at one end of the woodland while I ran across to the other end. In retrospect it was quite a hilarious moment; the deer standing on a woodland path with Kathy at one end and me at the other. The deer looked at both of us, sized up the situation and misguidedly decided that Kathy was her best option. There were a few seconds pause and then the deer charged towards Kathy. To my amazement she flew at the deer, tacked it and brought it to the ground. I raced towards them thinking to myself "Go girl! Don't let her go!"

I needn't have worried. Kathy did an amazing job. I honestly couldn't believe that she had tackled the deer and brought her down. It takes a lot of guts to do that. No wonder she ended up my girlfriend!

It's well known in wildlife rescue work that relationships can prove very difficult. The amount of dedication and time required is huge, and trying to get time off for relaxation and family can at times be impossible. Anyone thinking of getting involved with a wildlife rescuer - think twice! The antisocial hours, the tiredness, lack of regime, lack of money, unable to take a holiday during the summer, all cause problems. I've had my fair share of arguments as a result of tiredness. I've lost two girlfriends so far and I hope not to make it a hat trick. Fortunately Kathy is as involved in and as committed to our rescue work as me. She now heads up our hedgehog over-wintering; is our Volunteer Co-ordinator, a trustee, and always willing to get her hands dirty when there is no one else available. Not only is she brilliant with wildlife, she is also a dab hand at a bit of DIY; tiling the kitchen areas, painting the centre numerous times since we opened, and much more. She moans when the phone rings at 2am like we all do, but once awake she is always willing to go out and help with a rescue if needed. She has been a godsend. Wildlife rescue is not a profession or hobby you can pick up and put down as you wish, it's a long term commitment which will ruin your social life.

Whilst many people were on their way to parties and night clubs late on a Friday night, Tony and I were being called out by East Sussex Fire and Rescue Service to B&Q in Newhaven. There was a pheasant trapped in their warehouse that if not caught, would set off all the alarms. So the staff had called out Newhaven Fire and Rescue Service who, having spent about an hour trying and failing to catch the bird, decided to call us for help.

The pheasant was roosting on a beam about 20-30 feet up in the air. After a bit of head scratching I realised that there was going to be only one way to get it down, and it was not going to be easy for us or the pheasant.

A couple of firemen armed themselves with a thermal vision camera and a piece of timber while Tony and I armed ourselves with nets. A ladder was manoeuvred into place beneath the bird. All the store lights were switched off sending both bird and rescuers into pitch black. The timber was then used to disturb the

pheasant from its roost, but as the fireman could not see it in the dark, the thermal image camera was used to locate the bird.

The pheasant had no choice but to fly from the beam. Unable to see the other perches or beams, and after hitting a couple of lightweight hanging banners, the pheasant was unable to sustain its height and after a few seconds came down into one of the aisles. We could not just turn the lights on or the pheasant would simply fly back up to the beams again, so the firemen used the camera again to search for the bird.

We eventually found it clinging to the top shelf of one of the paint aisles— clearly wishing he was outside painting the town red rather than being stuck inside the store.

We managed to net it and take it back to WRAS's Centre where it was bedded down for the night. As there was nothing wrong with it, apart from possible wounded dignity, the following day we released it onto the neighbouring nature reserve.

On the 3rd November 2008 readers of the Hailsham Gazette voted for WRAS to receive a donation of £1000 from Tesco as part of the launch and opening of its new local store. WRAS Directors Sue, Murrae and I attended and we were presented with a cheque and cut a ribbon in front of the store. I was amazed that out of all the organisations and people who could have been chosen to open the store it was us!

Christmas Day 2008 saw Kathy and I attend a call to a hedgehog caught up in netting on a school field in Eastbourne. The finders had already cut it free and taken it home, but the remnants of the net were still attached to it. We managed to uncurl the hedgehog, remove the rest of the net and check it over for injuries. Luckily it was fine and as it was late in the day the finder agreed to release it later in the evening. Sadly a few days later we received a call about another hedgehog in the same netting. This time it was still trapped and we went to assess it. After cutting it free and checking it over, we looked around and found the remains of another hedgehog and also a dead fox in the same area. What really saddened us was that these fatalities were completely unnecessary, and the animals would most likely have suffered long lingering deaths. In order to prevent further casualties, we pulled the netting out of the ground and cable tied it about 6 inches off the floor so that if any further hedgehogs came along they could walk underneath and avoid becoming entangled. We took photos and sent a letter to the school explaining what we had done and why, and also sent out letters to all the other local schools warning them of the dangers. I think many took notice, and it is great to see more and more nets being tied up off the ground when not in use.

I want to take a moment to remember a very special dog, Jessie and her equally special owner, Mayke. They were both frequent visitors to the vets in Hailsham when Jessie was ill, and as I was often bringing in wildlife casualties we got to know each other. Mayke owned a company called Lavender and Sage and after her beloved dog passed away she set up "Jessie's Day" in her memory. Every year on Jessie's birthday, Mayke decided to donate her company's profits to the Kit Wilson Trust and WRAS. Although Mayke has now retired from Lavender and Sage she still supports WRAS, and over the years since Jessie died we have received over £8,000 in donations.

If it wasn't for the big-heartedness of people like Mayke, and so many others who give so generously, WRAS would not be where it is today and many of our native birds and mammals might be in a much poorer state or have suffered long and lingering deaths.

Chapter 13 - A fresh start and new beginnings.

At the end of 2008 we had no choice but to move out of our small set up at the vets' in Hailsham. The costs were rocketing way beyond our means. Our current paid manager was supposed to spend 30% of his time bringing in funds, but despite constant promises, this wasn't happening.

Quite quickly we managed to find new premises in a small industrial building at Whitesmith where we took one of the units and installed our cages and equipment. The site is owned by Anna and Bruce, a couple of our most generous supporters who offered us a great discounted rate. Simon Harris, the locum vet with whom we'd been working in Hailsham, agreed to come on board as our Veterinary Consultant. We then registered with the Royal College of Vets as a Veterinary Practice in order to be able to buy our own drugs and keep them on site and to save money. After seeking advice from the RCVS we agreed that it was best not to have the dangerous or controlled drugs at the unit; these would be kept by the vet, but basic pain relief, wormers, antibiotics and some other drugs we would store. As Simon was a locum vet, and not always in our area, the RCVS asked us to find a second, local vet to help with more urgent work. We had a good relationship with vet Chris Hall at Henley House Veterinary Surgery in Uckfield and he kindly agreed to step in and help support us.

Establishing our new centre was not going to be easy. Taking on more casualties meant taking on more facilities, which in turn means a greater need for additional volunteers and funding. But how to you do that? Where do you get them from? How do you manage them? Are they going to be reliable? What happens if they don't turn up? Do I need insurance? Should I be paying petrol expenses? What level of commitment can I ask of them? Do they need some form of training? Too many questions!

I contacted a number of organisations for advice and guidance. A number of which said stay small and manageable, and warned me how difficult things would get and explained some of the problems we would face.

I was very relieved when Kathy kindly stepped up and agreed to help take on the Volunteer Co-ordinator Role, as this was something which really worried me. I couldn't do everything on my own and risk getting ill again.

I'd seen too many people burn themselves out and I was determined this would not happen.

We decided to set up what we called the Feed & Clean Shifts. Some centres have volunteers who work all day continually feeding and cleaning. We decided we wanted the feeding and cleaning to be twice a day but to be undertaken quickly so there was plenty of quiet time throughout the day when the casualties can relax without the buzz of people being about. The role was set up initially for just two volunteers to work only 2 hours . This has slowly grown to be 4-5 volunteers working up to 3-4 hours twice a day with the morning shift starting about 9am and the evening shift after 5pm.

This role might not sound very important or special but it is vital. If the casualties are not fed, watered, and cleaned out properly they won't recover. These volunteers are a vital and extremely important part of the rehabilitation process – I don't think they realise just how important they are!

A couple of months later, Sussex Police made an unusual arrest in Eastbourne. It was a long eared owl. It had been found by scenes of crime officers. According to the RSPB long eared owls are not normally found in East Sussex. The bird had a damaged wing after being hit by a vehicle and because of its rarity, St Tiggywinkles Wildlife Hospital agreed to take it in and try to save its wing. Sadly the wing could not be fixed, but they have kept the owl which they use as part of a breed and release programme.

May 2009 saw another rare rescue; a deer with its antlers caught in a rope swing at Mayfield. It wasn't the rescue that was unusual, but the deer which turned out to be a very rare albino fallow deer. Kathy and Tony joined me in the attempt to disentangle it, a manoeuvre that turned out to be a huge challenge. The stag was running around on the top of a large embankment with a drop of about 20-30ft to a stream below.

Using a walk-towards net we managed to dodge between the trees and the thrashing deer and pin it to the trunk of a tree where it slid to the ground. I then spread-eagled myself over the deer to keep him steady on the ground whilst Tony and Kathy cut the rope free from the antlers. This took about

10 minutes. They then backed away and I slid backwards off the deer allowing it to jump up and spring off into the woodland.

This was the first time I had been called out to a true albino deer. The nose, eyes and even the deer's hooves were a red colour, while the rest of it was pure white. Such a beautiful and rare animal! Frequently very light coloured deer are seen and appear white, but are actually leucistic animals. Leucistic is a zoological term meaning having whitish fur, plumage, or skin due to a lack of pigment. Many people mistake leucistic animals for being albino but these creatures do not have the classic red eyes of an albino. Due to the lack of melanin production in both the retinal pigmented epithelium (RPE) and iris, albinos typically have red eyes due to the underlying blood vessels showing through. In contrast, most leucistic animals have normally coloured eyes.

Not long after this BDMLR asked me if I would drive down to Portsmouth to meet a white coated grey seal pup which was coming over by ferry from Jersey. Unfortunately there are no facilities on Jersey to take in and treat seals. They are normally sent across to Cornwall or Somerset but due to the high numbers of seal pups dealt with that year they didn't have room. So the next option was to get it to the RSPCA facilities at Mallydams Wood at Hastings, where there are purpose built facilities for seals.

Kathy and I met the ferry at Portsmouth, along with Jacqui who had travelled down from St. Tiggywinkles to gain experience, and BDMLR's Isle of Wight Co-ordinator Stephan. My job was to tube the seal with a rehydration fluid at the harbour, following BDMLR's guidelines for the transportation of seals. This involved catching the seal, securely holding its muzzle, inserting a tube down its throat and pouring in vital rehydration fluids. It might not sound nice, but it is crucial to the seal's welfare. His temperature was checked and found to be a little low, so we gave him a heat pad after his soiled bedding had been changed for some nice fluffy vet bed. After a break, to allow him to settle into his container and to recover from the long ferry ride, we then set off on the 90 mile journey to the RSPCA centre.

I was still experiencing problems within WRAS. I became stricter and more firm with our manager. I found myself being the victim of numerous malicious rumours. It was a very upsetting and distressing time. It had been agreed with our manager that £1000 would be raised within 4 weeks. At the next committee meeting I found that nothing had been raised. I became so distressed with the politics that I left the keys to the ambulance and the phones on the table and walked out. A short while later, our chairperson, Sue, came and found me and managed to talk me into staying. I agreed on the following condition; there would be a big shake up of how the organisation worked and that people would start taking responsibility for both their actions and the well-being of the charity.

A week later we held a meeting at which I laid everything down on the table. The manager resigned and several members also decided to step down. I stepped up and took over the reins of the charity, the rescue co-ordination, casualty management and fundraising.

To help kick-start the charity again, I gave WRAS the remainder of my savings. Our aim was a clean break and fresh start, but I knew that I had no choice but to be more careful with my health and limit my hours. From going so far backwards I aimed to push WRAS forwards again.

For several months we had to limit what we could take in, and work within our budgets very carefully. Kathy and I started paying for our own petrol in the ambulances, for some of the animal's food and, on one occasion, even some vets' bills. It was the only way we could rebuild the charity and get it back on its feet. Kathy and I were not prepared to stand by and watch something that we'd worked so hard for fall on its face. Between us we started doing most of the feed and clean shifts ourselves, and volunteers Les and Lillian also put in numerous long hours and were a great support to us through this time.

Slowly bit by bit over the summer months and into the winter WRAS started rising up again. We ran an appeal for funds, and donations came flooding in. The support we received was incredibly reassuring.

On the 18th October 2009 Kathy and I were called out after reports of a fallow deer caught in a fence off a footpath at Danehill. It was almost dark when we arrived and we were very surprised to see such a small baby deer, probably just a few days old, as fallow deer are usually born by the end of July. She had managed to get her head and both front legs through a square of stock fencing and her rear

legs were caught in the square below. It was clear she had been stuck there for a while.

After cutting away the wire I wrapped her in my jacket and carried her up to the ambulance where Kathy took over. We took her to a couple in Chelwood Gate who had experience in rearing baby deer. Due to being stuck for so long, she had internal injuries which had caused Haemorrhagic Enteritis, as well as external ligature injuries which left her with a scar and white fur in a circle around her tummy. We called her "Button", and were amazed at how well they did with her. Although it was touch and go for a long time, little by little she started to recover. To have a baby born at that time of year is very unusual when they should be being born early summer. She was certainly a little miracle, not least because she was born so unusually late in the season, and it also goes to prove that when dealing with any animal caught in stock fencing or any other entanglement where pressure is applied to the body, you should not just cut them free and release them. It is quite likely the animal will have suffered internal injuries that need to be treated to ensure there is some hope for survival, rather than a painful and lingering death.

Baby Button went on to develop into a fully grown deer and was released back to the wild, but she often returned to her foster parents' garden and, much to everyone's delight, the following year she gave birth to her own baby and came back to show her off.

This was followed by another deer rescue. Kathy and I were called out by the Kit Wilson Trust at Hadlow Down after a report of a stag with its antlers caught in wire. Unfortunately a passer-by had already cut the wire leaving the deer trailing a long piece of wire and wood. Volunteers from the Kit Wilson Trust had gone in search of the deer, as it was highly likely it would become entangled again and this time probably not in an area where it would easily be discovered until it was too late. When we arrived we started looking across the field and into the neighbouring woodland. Amazingly, the stag had managed to get over a fence but then the wire became attached to an old tree stump. These stag rescues are never easy, and when they have a large set of antlers they certainly make you think twice before jumping in.

Picking my moment I did my usual deer tackle and secured the deer. I quickly grabbed hold of the antlers to stop them hurting anyone and asked one of the Trust's staff to hold and secure the rear half of the deer. He certainly wasn't giving up without a fight!   Rapidly Kathy and other staff from the Kit Wilson Trust started cutting the wire and removing it from the deer's antlers.   As far as these rescues go this was one of the easier entanglements to remove. We were able to jump off and release the deer back to the wild and to freedom.

WRAS has never just been a taxi service for wildlife casualties. We have always tried to start the first aid and treatment of casualties out on site. 2009 saw a good example of this. We were called out to a swan hidden in long grass at the side of a lane crossing the Pevensey Levels.   The caller described to me how they had heard a commotion the other side of the field, had seen a dog charging off and an owner shouting and screaming at the dog. A short while later when walking past where the commotion took place, the caller noticed blood on the road and across the grass and then spotted a swan stuck in the long grass covered in blood. We gave this call a high priority and rushed to the scene. The swan was caught quite easily, but as soon as the swan moved its wing it started pumping out blood. We quickly applied a trauma gauze and pressure pad and held in place by Kathy in the back of our ambulance. We couldn't see exactly where the blood was pumping from due to the amount of tissue damage. Kathy accompanied the swan back to our Casualty Centre holding the pressure pad in place for the entire journey. The wound stopped bleeding, but we knew that any wrong moves and it could start again. After further treatment at our centre the swan was then rushed up to the Swan Sanctuary for their vets to work on.

It turned out that the unfortunate swan was going through a moult and was unable to fly and get away quickly enough from the dog. I have always believed that no dog should be off the lead if it can't be controlled.

Our first winter at the Shaw Barn turned out to be a tough one. We hadn't thought about what to do when it snowed. Worried that we would not be able to get to the centre in order to medicate, clean and feed the casualties, we decided that the only option was to stay overnight. During that winter of 2008/9 heavy snow caused major problems on the roads meaning many of our volunteers could not get in. I ended up staying overnight for 3 nights in a row and new WRAS committee members Brian and Monica took over at the weekend. It was not the most comfortable experience. The concrete floor was very cold, and the little heaters we had were not very effective. Even had I been warmer and more comfortable, the resident casualties weren't exactly conducive to a peaceful night's sleep. The tawny owl in the top cage kept flapping; the hedgehogs would huff and puff and those with lung worm would start coughing. Come first light I would then find myself being showered with seeds that the feral pigeons were flicking out of their cage at me - I like to think they were just trying to share their breakfast. Neither was it pleasant turning over on the floor and finding myself lying on a hard dry pea from the pigeon's food. Luckily the roads soon started to clear and things got back to normal again.

At the beginning of 2010 it was clear that WRAS's centre was way too small and inadequate. So I spoke to our landlord Bruce, who happens to be one of our biggest supporters, and asked him if we could take on a little garage attached to the building. Instead he asked me if I wanted to see one of the units on the other side of the building. I was amazed and delighted at its size. It was just the job. But the question was; could we afford to take it on? Bruce decided that instead of continuing to make donations each year, as well as charging us rent, instead of his annual donation, he would reduce the rent. This seemed like a fair deal. We sat down and calculated out the figures for rates and other possible expenditure and worked out that in order to take on the new centre it would cost in the region of £30,000 to set up. We started an appeal for items to be donated and money to be raised. We were determined to get our new Casualty Care Centre off the ground.

Chapter 14 - Finally some rest for the wicked!

March 2010 saw WRAS take in its first fox cubs of that year's season. The first three came from Langney where builders were digging up a patio and disturbed mum. They had no idea she was under there until they started lifting up slabs of concrete when, much to their surprise, they found the three baby fox cubs.

Kathy and I sat with the lights off in the patio owner's kitchen looking out of the window watching and waiting for mum to return. The weather was dreadful, with very high winds and rain. We had put the cubs in a crate outside with some towels and heat pads to keep them warm and a cloth covering it. It must have been about 11pm when a vixen first appeared. She came up onto the patio but was very wary. The stormy winds were really making her nervous after the ordeal of her den being uncovered earlier in the day.

Several times she appeared but kept getting spooked; at 2am she disappeared. With torrential rain starting we had no choice but to bring in the cubs. We went back the following night but she did not show at all. Such a shame.

There was nothing for it but to take the cubs into care. We had started giving our casualties names; each month someone at the centre would suggest a theme, such as cartoon characters, film stars or pop singers. On the one hand it was fun, and on the other it gave us a good idea of when a particular animal had been brought in.

That month's theme was biscuits, so we called them "Cookie", "Fudge" and "Rocky" as it seemed appropriate to name them after various types of Foxes biscuits.

These three little biscuits needed feeding every two to three hours and were taken on by WRAS carer and committee member Monica Russell. She was able to take them into work with her at the hairdressers in Hailsham.

Two more cubs came in the following week. One had been handed in to a vets in Hampden Park who kept it for five days before contacting us. It was a real job trying to de-tame the cub as he had clearly been played with, given too much attention and kept on its own for too long. This one we named "Crinkle" and he joined "Rocky", "Cookie" and "Fudge" as they were a very similar size.

On 23rd March I received a call about a cub in Bexhill. Kathy and I shot across to assess the situation, and were amazed to find a very small, less than two hour old fox cub which still had his umbilical cord and placenta attached. I think mum must have been disturbed and ended up giving birth to him on the run as the baby had been found in the middle of a driveway. This had to be the youngest fox cub we had ever dealt with. Kathy sat with him on her lap warming him up slowly on the journey to Monica in Eastbourne. Taking on any baby mammal is not an easy task but trying to feed and rear a newly born or premature baby is very hard. Monica did an amazing job with little "Shortcake", as we had called him.

WRAS is very careful about rearing animals and although it is important to interact with very young ones, it is crucial to know when to cut off that contact and allow the animal to develop with its own kind. Young foxes are kept until August/September time and eventually soft released back to the wild. This is during the foxes' natural dispersal period. It is safer to release them at this time of year as the vixens will be less threatening towards other cubs that might get close to their own youngsters.

2010 turned into a very busy year. It was not just calls about wildlife that kept us occupied, we were receiving loads of calls about domestic and agricultural animals. On Monday 22nd March I received over twelve calls for help with a peahen wandering around Uckfield and seven turkeys on the loose in Alfriston. Sadly there doesn't seem to be an equivalent organisation in the area which deals with domestic and agricultural animals and the RSPCA is over stretched.

Other calls that came in were about a polecat in Seaford, cats stuck up trees, stray and abandoned dogs, missing parrots, escaped pet birds of prey, agricultural and pet sheep which have escaped, runaway snakes in peoples' houses, chickens fallen off lorries, chipmunks living wild and many more. We are a wildlife rescue charity and one of the problems with having become a registered charity is that we have to be careful that the Charities Commission doesn't fine us for working outside our remit. Our volunteers will, on certain occasions, help where they can and I and others have funded these rescues out of our own pockets. But money doesn't grow on trees and there are only 24 hours in a day.

Although there are a number of domestic animal centres in and around Sussex that do a fantastic job, they are sanctuaries and not rescue or ambulance services. The funding just isn't there for this service to be provided. When I first started doing rescue work I used to get frustrated by the RSPCA and other organisations not being able to help, but the demand way outstrips the capability and resources of such organisations to be able to respond to every call about a domesticated animal that's escaped, fallen off the back of a lorry or stuck up a tree.

Later in the Spring Kathy and I drove down to Lewes after receiving a couple of calls; some baby hedgehogs had been disturbed in a greenhouse and a couple of adders were entangled in pea netting on an allotment. We dealt with the baby hedgehogs first, collecting them and warming them up, before heading off to find the snakes.

When we arrived the snakes had already been cut out of the netting and placed in a box. They were two young female adders and pretty lively. As with any situation involving entanglement in netting or wire, ligature wounds can prove a serious health risk.

It's quite a delicate manoeuvre trying to check a snake, especially a poisonous one, and it's impossible to do when wearing thick gloves. So my tactic was to pick up an adder wearing thin latex gloves, grasp it firmly, and then check for any signs of damage. The first one was fine and but the second one, a particularly frisky little snake, was determined to break free. Very stupidly, and without thinking, instead of putting the snake back in the box and re-capturing it carefully and firmly, I swapped hands allowing it the freedom to sink its fangs through my latex gloves into my hand. Various people in the reptile world were not backwards at coming forwards with a fair degree of criticism, which I would accept, although in my defence it's really not possible to check a snake for ligature wounds with heavily gloved hands. But it was my own silly mistake, and given what came next, not one I am likely to repeat.

I finished off my assessment and the snakes were all fine, so the allotment holders were asked to take them back to their plots and release them. As with any bite from wildlife we get the injury checked out at the local hospital. So Kathy and I drove the short distance to Lewes's Minor Injury Unit. We waited for about a quarter of an hour before being seen. But during those fifteen minutes I started developing severe back pain. The nurse was unsure what to do so phoned Brighton Hospital for advice. The hospital asked if I could make my way to them

for an assessment. The pain in my back was getting rapidly worse. I stood up and then suddenly just passed out on the floor as my blood pressure plummeted. All I can remember after that was someone saying my name and the sound of sirens, until I woke up in the resuscitation ward at Brighton Royal Sussex County Hospital.

It was not till the following day, when one of the Paramedics came in to see how I was doing, that I was told the full story about what happened. He also wanted to write up the case for future reference.

Apparently, after my collapse, the nurse at Lewes Hospital called for paramedics. When they arrived they had to work on me for some twenty minutes before they could get any pulse or blood pressure readings from my right arm. They then rushed me by ambulance to Brighton's Accident and Emergency Department where I was taken to resuscitation. They called in a doctor who had previous experience with snake bites. He gave me anti-venom along with numerous other drugs.

WRAS volunteers Monica and Brian kindly came across to be with Kathy and to take care of the baby hedgehogs we'd rescued earlier that day. At about 7pm I was conscious enough for visitors and they were shown in to see me. I still had little real idea about what had gone on and was more worried about ensuring all the animals were safe and sorted out back at our centre than I was about a little snake bite. It was only when Kathy told me that she had been warned by the doctors that I may not survive, that the seriousness of the situation hit home.

Nurses observed my condition overnight in the Acute Care Ward and I was then allowed to return home at 6pm on the Sunday. My fingers, hands and right arm were swollen, as well as the lymph glands under my right arm.

The doctor recommended complete rest for at least ten days, but in any case the pain and restricted movements in my arms meant that I was unable to drive for at least that amount of time, so no more rescues for me for a while.

It was good to have a bit of a break, but this was not the type of break I was really after. For the first few days I was very tired and slept a lot. But then I started to get bored and needed to do something. I came up with the idea of making a wildlife train set model that incorporated various wildlife hazards for use at events. It was actually great fun and a good diversion seeking out bits and pieces to re-create hazardous netting, broken stock fencing, litter, people fishing near swans, shooting deer, people digging a badger sett and more. The end result is still very much in use when I take it to various schools or events. Both children and adults seem to love it.

I would like to take this opportunity to thank the nurses at Lewes Minor Injury Unit, the Paramedics as well as the Doctors and Nurses at the Royal Sussex County Hospital's A&E department, Re-sus and Acute Care Ward for their expert care and attention in looking after me so well. It cannot have been easy and it was certainly very frightening for Kathy, Brian and Monica being told that I might not make it. I really appreciate them for being there for me. I am most grateful for the help and support from all the WRAS volunteers, and especially David who was temporarily working for WRAS, funded by a Royal British Legion employment scheme.

I certainly don't want people to read this and start worrying about snakes in their gardens. Less than one in five adder bites inject enough venom to cause any problems; normally the first bite is a warning. In situations like the one I found myself dealing with, the rescuers are more at risk than people who encounter them under normal circumstances would be.

I was told by my doctor that I should no longer deal with adders as the anti-venom should really only be given once due to side effects. Kathy has also ordered me not to deal with any more or she will kill me herself next time!

It was not long after this that I received a couple of phone calls about hedgehogs that had been injured as a result of being kicked. The first was found in the public area of Uckfield Community College, the second was less than a week later and was found on a footpath leading to the footbridge crossing the railway just east of Lewes Railway Station. This had been found by students from Priory School in Lewes who very kindly looked after the hedgehog and protected it until I arrived in our Ambulance.

The Uckfield hedgehog had suffered a damaged spine, trauma to the lungs, trauma to the nasal cavity, a fractured leg and had breathing difficulties. The Lewes hedgehog suffered eye and ear injuries, swelling and bruising to the face, three fractures to the upper jaw as well as trauma to the nasal cavity. Both hedgehogs had to be euthanized as a result of their injuries. These were some of the worst cases of animal cruelty I have come across. As a result we issued a press release and wrote to the local schools. Rescuer David and I spent the next two mornings handing out flyers outside the two schools that requested help in catching those responsible and making people aware of the incidents.

Another sad incident, but this one with a happy ending, was at Maresfield. A gentleman phoned us to say he'd shot a partridge with his air rifle, mistaking it for a rabbit. I jumped into our ambulance and was there within 20 minutes to find he had already picked up the bird. There were quite extensive swellings around its head and bleeding from one eye. The partridge was assessed by vet, Chris Hall, at Henley House Vets and given an x-ray to check for a pellet. Luckily the pellet appeared to have hit the cheek bone and bounced off, but the extensive swelling around the head meant partridge couldn't see anything as he could not open his eyes. After about four days the swelling subsided, the partridge started improving, could open his eyes and became much perkier. After a couple of weeks care, the partridge was well enough to be released and returned to the garden. The owner vowed to be more careful in future! I told him he shouldn't be shooting rabbits in the first place. At this same property WRAS has since been called to three deer, two caught in stock fencing and another collapsed in the garden.

On Easter Sunday 2010 WRAS had planned to have a stand at the Sussex Horse Rescue's Grand Open Day at Uckfield. However Sussex Police phoned us asking if we could deal with two boars found roaming around Kingston village near Lewes. They had tried various organisations but couldn't find anyone to help.

When I arrived I was surprised at how big they were, at about five foot in length. They were clearly not wild boar, but none the less we decided to be very cautious. They had some horrible injuries to their ears where ear tags had probably been ripped out, were clearly underweight and had some old injuries to their bodies. There was no way I was going to be able to catch them on my own. So I phoned Kathy and asked if she would speak to Pauline at the Horse Rescue and ask for her help. Pauline was already greeting visitors at their open day when Kathy approached her about the boar, but she did not hesitate in coming over to help with their horse box.

The male boar was quite calm and clearly more interested in the food we threw down than by anything else, and was quickly rounded up into the horse box. The female, however, was much more frightened and wary, probably due to an injury to her shoulder and ear. Accompanied by a local resident and neighbouring farmer, it took us about two hours to catch her. I ended up getting scratched to bits trying to get in the bushes and encourage her in the right direction.

Once loaded into the horse box they were driven back to Sussex Horse Rescue Trust's sanctuary at Hempstead Lane, Uckfield, in the middle of their Grand Open Day and left to settle down after their ordeal, away from the visitors.

Kathy, Pauline and I managed to get back to the Horse Rescue Sanctuary just in time to meet TV celebrity cleaner, Kim Woodburn, from "How Clean is your House?" who was visiting the sanctuary.

We could not have rescued the boar without the support of Sussex Horse Rescue Trust, and I am very grateful to them for their help. WRAS does not normally respond to these types of calls. From talking to local residents it appears that they had been wandering around the village since the previous

Wednesday, about the same time WRAS was called about some turkeys that were spotted roaming around on the edge of Kingston and Lewes.

The two boar quickly settled in to their temporary home at Uckfield. A few weeks later they were found permanent quarters with new owners in Kent who have vowed to take care of them and not eat them!

In September 2010 we were delighted to announce that Sarah Jane Honeywell from Cbeebies, had agreed to be a new Patron for WRAS.

Sarah Jane is well known for her work as a comedy actress and kids TV presenter, but perhaps what is less well known is that she is a vegan and a passionate animal lover.

At the beginning of August, in advance of opening our Casualty Centre at Whitesmith, she came to Sussex to see for herself the work we do.

We initially met up in Ashdown Forest so she could be introduced to Caramel, the baby deer recently rescued in Crowborough and much to our surprise and delight, Button and Billie, two of the previous year's baby deer happened to drop by to pay us a visit.

After lunch we took her to Kathy's garden in Uckfield to meet some of the young hedgehogs who were in soft release pens getting acclimatized to outdoor life before being freed back to the wild. Sarah Jane was enchanted by "Tic Tac" - the first hedgehog she had ever held.

We then visited our new centre at Whitesmith to see how the work was progressing, and to meet some of the WRAS volunteers. Finally Sarah Jane followed us up to East Grinstead's Moat Pond where she helped us release a young duck that we had rescued the previous day, having become entangled in fishing line and hooks.

It was a great day for us all at WRAS, and I think Sarah Jane not only enjoyed herself and loved meeting the animals, but she also seemed very impressed by the work we do.

Chapter 15 - The WRAS Community Grows.

The summer of 2010 continued to be very busy. WRAS was receiving up to 3,000 calls a year. Hardly a day went by without multiple calls-outs and night time rescues were now regular occurrences. I was still working for British Divers Marine Life Rescue and my time and energy were stretched so thinly I came to the conclusion that something had to give. I needed to work at either BDMLR or WRAS full time. One of them would have to be sacrificed. Although I had helped pull WRAS back together over the previous few years it certainly was not rich enough to employ me. I sat down and had a very open and frank conversation with Alan Knight, the Chairman of BDMLR and International Animal Rescue, (and by then Alan Knight OBE), and expressed my concerns. I put together a proposal for International Animal Rescue to fund my wage at £800 a month so I could work for WRAS, leave BDMLR and let someone else take over who had more time to dedicate to the national role.

After a few meetings I was delighted that IAR agreed to fund £600 a month. WRAS's trustees and committee members agreed to subsidize the remaining £200. I finally started working full time for WRAS, albeit on a part time wage.

On Saturday 4th September 2010 Sarah Jane Honeywell, with the assistance of Hellingly Brownie Pack, officially opened WRAS's new Casualty Care Centre at Whitesmith. Phase One was complete. The casualties had moved in!

When we had first taken on the unit back in April, the empty shell was a mess. Rubbish, old tools, paint tins, an old engine, pots of chemicals and thick dust were everywhere. The entry doors were rotten at the bottom and little furry friends were getting in underneath, leaving their tell-tale footprints all over the place. We had decided that it would be in the casualties' best interest to move into the larger building so they could be provided with better facilities. It would be less crowded, less noisy and easier for the volunteers to work in.

On the 1st April WRAS took possession of the keys and made a start developing the new centre. Our volunteers worked very hard cleaning up, painting the unit from top to bottom and even constructing partition walls to reduce costs. The contractors were asked to make safe the electrics, plaster the internal walls, sort out the plumbing and install the new flooring. Once that was done, our volunteers again did us proud; painting, installing recycled cupboards, laying floor tiles up-stairs, putting in a new entry door, internal windows and doors and moving in the old caging and equipment. It was a transformation. When I look back at the pictures I can't believe it is the same building.

The downstairs was made up of seven sections; a food preparation and cleaning area, a treatment room, two casualties rooms, an isolation room, as well as a wet room and large animal area that was still under construction. Upstairs was divided into five areas; the main central room for educational use and meetings, the volunteers' kitchen, staff room, an office plus a toilet.

Over sixty guests attended the opening and allowed limited access to the hospital area, to avoid causing stress to the casualties. Sarah Jane Honeywell presented WRAS volunteers Dick, Tony, Les, Keith and Steve with bottles of wine as a thank you for all their hard work and Kathy received a beautiful bouquet of flowers. We in turn gave Sarah Jane a framed set of photos of her visit to WRAS, including her meeting with Button the deer and Tic-Tac the hedgehog. We had a great celebration with refreshments and food, all provided by WRAS and its volunteers, including my infamous butternut squash and ginger soup.

The work on the centre was by no means finished and very much in need of further alterations and additional caging - all of which was going to require considerable fundraising.

A couple of weeks after the opening of the centre, Kathy and I had a holiday of a lifetime. I had not been on a proper holiday in over 20 years.

It came completely out of the blue. One evening we were having dinner with one of our major donors when he offered us the use of his villa on Grand Bahama. It was so tempting, but the reality was that we didn't have the money to get there.

A week later he asked me if we had thought seriously about it. I told him that we just couldn't afford to go as the flights were too expensive, to which he said "Don't worry about those, I'm happy to cover the costs of you getting there and hiring a car". Kathy and I were gobsmacked! We really didn't know whether we should accept or not; we felt guilty about accepting such a generous donation that could have gone to WRAS. I asked a few friends for advice and all of them had the same response, "Do it! This is a once in a life time opportunity, don't miss it!"

So we went, just for a week. We had been offered longer, but with so much work needing to be done at our new centre we really couldn't afford to spend any more time away.

But what a week it was! Swimming in the blue sea, walking along the white sand to the beach bar and drinking rum, plus visiting the national parks where we saw so many different birds and wildlife. I wasn't too keen on the spiders, but the scenery and wildlife were breath-taking. We entered one cave and to our amazement a bat flew round and up the stairs we had just walked down. We had a terrific time and a holiday that Kathy and I will never forget. Neither will we forget extraordinary generosity. Thank you!

2010 saw me start my 25th year as a wildlife rescuer. In October I was invited to the House of Lords to receive a prestigious Animal Action Award from the International Fund for Animal Welfare. The ceremony, hosted by Baroness Gale, was also attended by Eastbourne MP Stephen Lloyd. Kathy and I were accompanied by Alan Knight and fellow committee members Brian and Monica. Also receiving awards were another wildlife rehabber, Caroline Gould, from Vale Wildlife Rescue in Gloucestershire and the wildlife lover, rock star and astronomer, Brian May.

As if getting one award wasn't enough, I was then invited to the Sovereign FM Radio Awards 2010 in the Grand Hotel, Eastbourne. The event was packed with many other deserving people, and I was totally dumbfounded when I was presented with the Life Time Achievement Award. I really didn't feel I had done anything different from so many other people in the area.

Towards the end of the year I was called out to a heron that had become ensnared on a pond at Palehouse Common near Uckfield. When I arrived I could hear a strange tinkling, ringing sound long before I could see the heron.

Its wings and legs were entangled in the string and mechanics of a wind chime that had been hanging over the garden pond; this accounted for the strange noise I had heard as the bird struggled to free itself. It took a bit of doing but eventually I managed to corner the heron and catch it so I could disentangle it. I covered the bird's head to avoid being stabbing by its long, sharp beak.

The metal parts of the wind chime were fairly simple to remove but cutting it free from the string was not at all easy. A lot of the string was now underneath the feathers making it extremely difficult to find and cut.

After about twenty minutes the bird was eventually sorted. With no sign of ligature wounds I climbed on top of the nearby shed and threw the bird into the air. To my relief and delight it took off, flew across the field, over to nearby woodland and safety.

2011 was yet another busy year. Kathy and I spent a lot of time recruiting and training new volunteers to help with different roles. At the same time we were also answering the constantly ringing phone, writing newsletters and grant applications, organising events as well as co-ordinating and attending rescues.

One newly recruited volunteer was Karen who worked at a barbers shop in Eastbourne. She was incredibly enthusiastic and set up a "just giving" page on the internet, raising money by running nine marathons in nine weeks. She collected over £800 for WRAS, a remarkable achievement.

We were also donated a really good microscope that enabled us to give our casualties even better treatment. With the completion of our first aid room, the microscope has proved invaluable, especially when analysing potential problems with over-wintering hedgehogs.

With guidance and training from vet Simon Harris, and from Vale Wildlife Rescue, we were able to start identifying various parasites and therefore target medication more accurately. Previously, if a hedgehog was unwell,

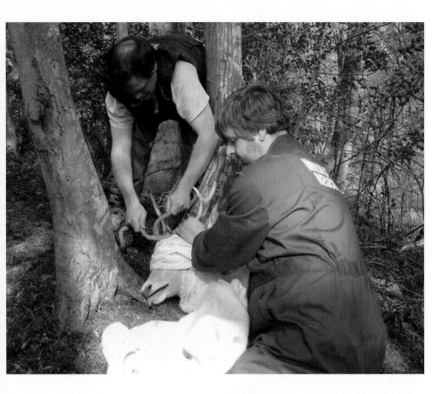

Above: Trevor holds on tightly to an albino fallow deer whilst rescuer Tony cuts the rope from the deer's antlers. Below: The albino deer at the top of a slope in Mayfield with its antlers entangled in a childs woodland rope swing.

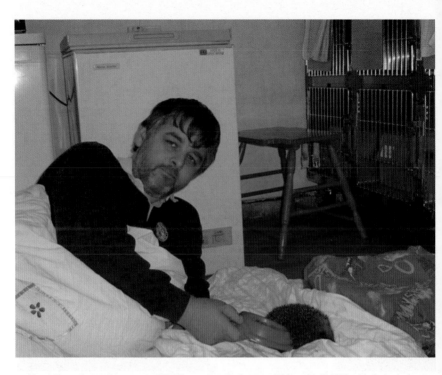

Above: Trevor has to sleeps over at WRAS's new Casualty Centre at Whitesmith, in 2009, with the hedgehogs during the winter snow fall in case rescue . Below: Trevor tubes the white coat Grey Seal at Portsmouth Harbour.

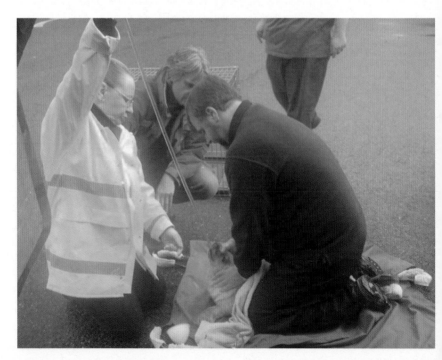

Above: The abandoned domestic Boar rescued at Kingston near Lewes – insert at the Sussex Horse Rescue Centre. Below: Trevor's swollen hand and the two Adders which bit Trevor, putting him in hospital.

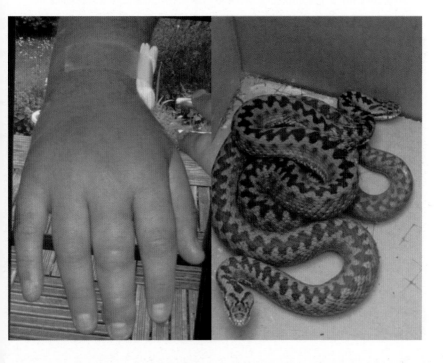

Above: 1st April 2010 WRAS took on the keys for the new Centre. The site was a mess and needed lots of work. Below: July 2010, volunteers help paint and decorate the new Prep Room area.

Above: Actress Sarah Jane Honeywell cuts the bandage and opens WRAS's new Casualty Centre in September 2010 Below: Trevor with Vet Simon examining a badger in the new First Aid Room.

Above: Trevor being presented the Life Time Achievement Award at the Sovereign FM Awards 2010. Below: Trevor at the House of Lords for the IFAW Animal Action Awards in London in 2010.

Above: Kathy's legs sticking out of the fox's den whilst trying to rescue the Dallington Fox Cubs. Below Left: Kathy with one of the rescued cubs. Below Right: A camera was used to take photos inside the den to see where and how many fox cubs were inside.

Above Left: Trevor with a rescued abandoned badger cub at Friston Forest. Above Right: Rescuer Tony catches a crashed swan in Eastbourne. Below Left: A youing tawny owl is found sat on a log on a busy dog walking path at Battle. Below Right: Trevor replaces the baby Tawny Owl back in its nest to avoid being caught by dogs.

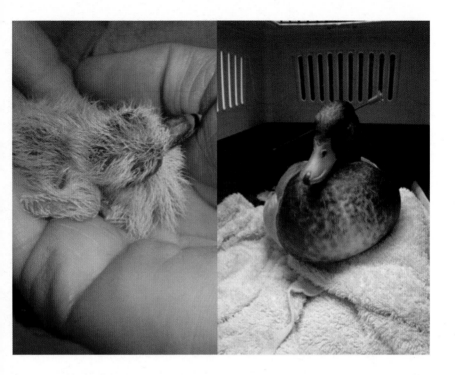

Above Left: A baby feral pigeon almost fresh from the egg, which Kathy hand reared. Above Right: "Dart Duck" rescued at the Pells Pond Lewes on New Years Eve with a 7 inch dart through its neck. Below: The Tawny Owl from Isfield Nursery School with inserts of the children's thank you card.

Above: The Pells Pond Swan which Trevor had to check on after receiving numerous reporting it to be stuck on ice. Above Right: On Intravenous fluids this fox was suspected of suffering from poisoning. Below Left: A starling rescued from a bat fall feeder. Below Right: Kathy with the pigeon rescued from Poundland.

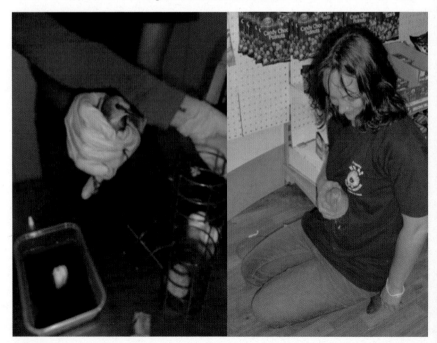

Above Left: Trevor and Kathy at Buckingham Palace 2012. Right: Trevor with his family and Stephen Lloyd MP for Eastbourne. Below: Trevor with Virginia McKenna OBE at the BBC Sussex Community Heroes Awards. Photo Courtesy of BBC Radio Sussex & Surrey.

Above Left: Filming for the Dick n Dom Go Wild Programme. Above Right: Trevor with Breakfast Television star Kate Garroway. Below: Trevor rescues a fox from Brambles and fencing at Willingdon Primary School.

Above Left: Manger Lindsay at Bodium Castle with a rescued duckling. Above Right: A rescued baby rabbit at WRAS. Below Left: Chris with Sherman the fox cub rescued from a Septic Tank. Below Right: "Paddy" an albino wild Hedgehog.

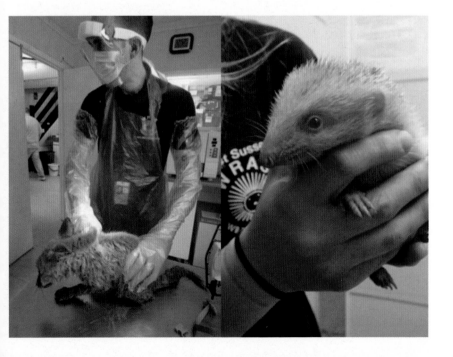

Above: Trevor vaccinating one of the first badger to ever be vaccinated in Sussex against bTB as part of the Sussex Badger Vaccination Project in 2014 in Uckfield. Below A soaked Trevor carries an injured swan back to the ambulance. Insert - the blood covered swan in need of rescue on the Pevensey Levels.

Above Left: Trevor sits on top of a 6ft high wall in Rottingdean, waiting for a hedgehog to come out of a pipe in the wall. Above Right: Kathy checks the hedgehog over once caught. Below: A Brown Long Eared bat rescued at Piltdown after being caught by a cat.

Above: Kathy and Trevor release a Roe Deer which was trapped at the top of a 40ft high ridge at Sand Ridge, Uckfield in 2015.

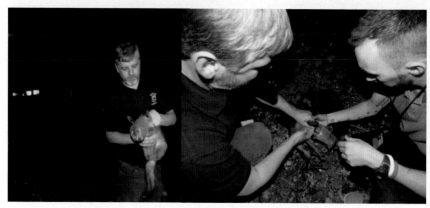

Above: Trevor and Chris rescuing a fox cub with its head stuck in a plastic pot in Eastbourne.
Below: A cartoon paid for by Karen in America to celebrate Trevor's 30th and WRAS's 20th Year helping wildlife in need.

we had to take an educated guess at which were the most likely parasites infecting it. If one medication didn't work we would try another, or we would have to take samples and pay to have them analysed. With the new microscope we were not only saving money, but also more accurately targeting the medication and speeding up treatment and recovery. You can tell a lot from microscopically examining at animals' poo, and when you get a group of wildlife rehabilitators in a room together it's not long before they are discussing faeces!

During the spring and summer we get extremely busy. There are some occasions when we are unable to return calls, and others when we are unable to help some callers and casualties, simply because of the work overload.

It is not because we can't be bothered or don't care, it is because physically and financially we can't. During these months our volunteers work very hard, sometimes round the clock on very little sleep. Sadly some callers can get quite aggressive and rude if we are unable to help even though we have apologised and pointed them in the direction of someone who can help, or suggested they try a local vet or call the national RSPCA.

Most do understand that we are only a small organisation with limited resources and funds; they are polite and usually satisfied with our advice. There are a few though, who get very disgruntled and try to use emotional blackmail, saying we don't care or can't be bothered, or they accuse us of only being interested in "special" species. I can understand that some people are very concerned about the casualties' welfare causing them to become upset and frustrated. But there are those who, no matter what we say, will always get angry with us and nothing will appease them apart from attending.

Occasionally I admit I have lost my temper. On one such occasion I had been up all night, finally getting to bed at 4am when, for my own sanity, switched on the answerphone. Our answerphone message suggests that if the caller doesn't hear back from us shortly, then if possible to take urgent casualties to the vets or to other organisations. We would rather this than have an injured animal wait ages for us to attend if we are unable to respond quickly.

A lady from Heathfield had called at 7am. She had been on her way to work and had come across an injured rabbit at the side of the road. I returned her call later in the morning and she told me that she had left the rabbit where she found it and was horrified that we had not yet dealt with it. I asked her, politely, if she could pop back and check to see if it was still there as we had quite a few calls to deal with and wanted to try and avoid driving all the way there only to find the rabbit had gone. She screamed down the phone at me telling me that was my job and I shouldn't be so lazy!

I calmly and diplomatically tried to explain that I had been up all night, but the lady just kept blaming us for leaving the rabbit. The conversation was going round in circles. I politely suggested that as she was closer she could have returned and picked up the rabbit herself and taken it to the local vets. It doesn't have to be us that take it in and this would have saved us a lot of time, especially as we were busy. I'm afraid this probably didn't come out quite as diplomatically or politely as I had intended. I was still exhausted. The result was the lady exploded; I lost my patience and hung up as it was clear the conversation was going nowhere. The upshot was that she called back several times and was less than civil.

On another occasion a small hotel owner had a right go at me because I refused to remove a swan from his lake that was becoming aggressive towards the guests. He demanded we come and move it. I explained why the swan was acting aggressively, and what could be done to avoid his guests having a problem, but he was still not happy. After receiving a mouthful of abuse from him, I put the phone down. A short while later, having spoken to the Swan Sanctuary, the hotel owner called again. He apologised telling me he hadn't realised we were a charity and genuinely thought we are part of the local council and paid for by his council tax. Which we are not by the way! But apology graciously given, and accepted.

I do what I do because I love animals, in particular the wild animals that don't have owners to look after them if they are sick or injured. I cannot bear to see any animal suffering. However, over the past twenty years I

146

have learnt that in order to be of most help, there have to be limits, and there have to be priorities, in order to prevent those involved burning themselves out.

There have been a few of our volunteers who believe we should never say no; that we should help every single person who calls. I have witnessed many of them leave WRAS to set up their own rescue organisations only for them to fold within a couple of years because they have over-stretched their resources. Our priority is always to look after the casualties we already have in care. If funding is low we have to ensure we can care for them first and foremost. As a result rescues have occasionally had to stop. Every casualty costs money; vets bills, electricity, water, waste, medication, phone bills, food, cleaning, bedding, fuel and more. Although we are very efficient, and have been congratulated on the amount we do on such a small budget, we don't have an endless pit of money.

If you don't have priorities and set limits when necessary, you run the risk of jeopardising the welfare of many, rather than just a few animals. If you look on the internet, you'll find plenty of examples of people who have overstretched themselves by an inability to say no. They become over-loaded, can't afford to look after the casualties and don't have the man power to do all the work. The result; standards and quality of care start slipping, and not just one, but all the casualties start to suffer.

By setting limits WRAS has grown from strength to strength and, in the long term, has managed to help more and more casualties. Saying no for a few weeks can mean you are then able to help casualties for the rest of the year. Saying yes all the time, it's odds-on that you'll have to shut down because you have gone bankrupt.

Charity politics tend to be a mine-field of potential arguments and pitfalls. Animal charities in particular seem to attract this more than most. There are those who have the attitude, "If you don't do it my way you must be doing it the wrong way." Sadly this mind-set can prevent groups from working together. There are always going to be multiple ways of dealing with things. If it works and doesn't cause any unnecessary distress, suffering or cause problems after release, then the procedure shouldn't be knocked. Having said that, I do believe that we should all be open to new ideas and constantly strive to develop our knowledge and ability to help wildlife in the best way possible.

Despite the negative sides to social media, Facebook has managed to bring a number of organisations like WRAS together. We share knowledge and information as well as unusual cases in order to help each other learn and develop.

However, you do see some horrendous pictures of well-meaning individuals who are not using vets, not using proper medication, or keeping animals and birds alive which are clearly suffering and need to be euthanized. One example I saw were pictures of a feral pigeon with both legs and wings broken and it had not been seen by a vet!

They say a little knowledge is dangerous, which is why you should always liaise and talk things over with those who have more experience. One of our advisers told us how she had a new carer who was looking after an African Pygmy Hedgehog with mites. She'd been advised to use Advocate (a recognised flea treatment). She called to say she was very worried as the mites weren't going away and the hedgehog's skin was getting worse. She then sent a photo. The hog looked weird; sort of yellowy coloured and shiny. Our advisor asked her new carer what she thought had caused it, and she replied that the only thing she had put on him was Advocate and he'd gone like that afterwards. So she was asked to bring in the hedgehog.

When he arrived there was a rather odd smell that seemed familiar and after a lot of confused questioning it turned out she'd used Advocaat! No wonder the mites hadn't gone, they were having a party!

Once on the right kind of medication the hedgehog returned to his normal colour and all was well. It was a salutary, if amusing, incident.

Early 2011 saw us dealing with a number of swan rescues. Just after Christmas we were called out to a swan with a broken wing at Newhaven Marina. Although the swan was swimming around the harbour, it spent most of its time by the slipway and could clearly be seen dragging a wing. I tried and failed to catch him from land as he was way too wary. Thanks to help from the local Newhaven Dive Club boat, we were able to go out onto the water and catch the swan that way, undoubtedly saving its life. We took him to the Swan Sanctuary at Shepperton for their vet to assess the wing. Unfortunately the wing was badly broken and had to be partially amputated. But the swan was offered a home at the sanctuary where he paired up with another disabled swan and they were both able to live out the rest of their lives, as if wild, on a private lake.

The next swan rescue was at Hailsham Common Pond. Some visitors were concerned about a swan with a lump in its neck. Often this is just caused by food, but you would normally see it slowly moving down the neck. The lump however was not moving so needed further investigation. Unlike the Newhaven swan, this patient was more co-operative and walked across the ice towards me or probably rather more enticingly, towards the bread I was proffering. I spent several minutes lulling the swan into a false sense of security and once settled, comfortable and close enough to reach, swiftly grabbed it and lifted it out of the water onto the bank. The lump clearly needed a closer examination so the swan was also taken to the Swan Sanctuary. Their vets found the lump to be an abscess, possibly caused by a fishing hook. After a small operation the swan made a full recovery and was returned to the pond.

Rescuers Sue and Tony also attended swans. A pair had misguidedly landed in a fenced off enclosure at the back of Tollgate School. The swans had spent over three hours trying to fly out, but the distance to the fence was too short for take-off, and each time they had to abort their attempt. They were never going to make it without help. In order to get to the swans Tony had to climb over a 7ft high gate. Having managed to catch them, he then had to climb back over the gate, a swan under each arm, and took them to the WRAS ambulance. Both swans were checked over and found to be in good health, if somewhat embarrassed by their unintended imprisonment in the school's grounds. They were released just along the road at Princes Park where they would have no problem achieving a successful take-off and continuing their journey.

In April 2011 I received a call from a horse rider who had found a baby fox cub wandering along a narrow lane. She placed the cub back into the nearby den where she saw another cub that was calling for its mother, and then noticed a dead adult fox and grew concerned for the cubs' welfare. Kathy and I went over to check the dead fox and discovered it was a lactating vixen that had been dead for about 24 – 48 hours and probably a road casualty. We could hear the cubs calling underground in a den at the side of the road. It was a difficult and frustrating rescue as we had to work on a steep bank right at the edge of the road. It was made even more difficult because the entrance tunnel turned a sharp 90 degrees to where the cubs were living. We used our camera to take photos so we could establish exactly where they were and the layout of the tunnel. We saw there were also two dead cubs in the tunnel. We had no choice but to use a spade to widen the entrance hole so we could reach round the corner to remove the dead cubs and access those that were still alive.

Alan Knight, who lives only a couple of miles away, came to our aid with a spade, cat food and vital life-saving fluids to help save the remaining cubs. Kathy, being the smallest of us, then had the job of wriggling inside and reaching round the bend to get to the cubs. She was able to reach the first at about 6.20pm, but the others had moved further down the tunnel making it impossible to get to them. So we decided the only thing we could do for the moment, was to back off.

Volunteers Debbie and Sam who as well as running their own rescue organisation from Rotherfield, also helped WRAS, arrived to take the first cub away for care and to get much needed food into him. This allowed us time to concentrate on rescuing the remaining orphans. After a short break we returned to the hole to find the cubs had moved closer to the entrance again.

As Kathy squeezed into the hole, one of the cubs came towards her, thinking she might be mum returning with food. Despite the lack of space to move easily, Kathy was able to grab cub number two. However she had squirmed so far into the hole that the only way to get her out was by pulling her legs with all my might. After a final tug, Kathy emerged covered in bruises and scratches but firmly clasping a hungry and thirsty little fox.

But the rescue wasn't quite over. Much to our surprise we noticed that there was a third cub, and after further gymnastic contortions Kathy managed to get number three. Certain that this was the last of the litter, the rescue finally ended at 9.30pm just as Debbie and Sam returned with hot coffee. They collected the cubs and took them home to be reunited with their brother.

This was a rescue that we really thought was going to end badly. There was no way that I was going to fit down the hole, and Kathy who is much slimmer than I, was heroic. The orphans were all dehydrated, underweight and starving. There was no chance they could have lasted another 24 hours and would have suffered a horrible, slow death. There was also no way that we would have been able to sleep that evening, knowing the cubs were there and most likely dead by the morning. We were so glad all our hard work had paid off, although we laughed that Kathy, scratched and bruised as she was, wasn't going to be wearing any summer dresses for a while.

With the set-up of the new Casualty Centre I had the unforgiving task of trying to bring more funds in to help cover the costs. Frequently I found I was being told that as we are an animal charity we are not eligible for grant funding or donations because, apparently, we don't benefit humans or the community.

While obviously WRAS's main concern is to help wild animals that cannot help themselves, in so doing I fervently believe that we are also "benefitting humans and the community".

It is not the animals that call WRAS's 24 hour rescue-line, it is the humans. Humans, who care about sick and injured animals and like us, do not want to see any animal suffer. While our primary concern is to attend to the wildlife, we also provide peace of mind to those who find them. When confronted with a sick, injured or orphaned animal and with no wherewithal or expertise to help them, people can suffer anxiety, stress, anger, panic and many other upsetting emotions. This is especially so during the night when many veterinary centres are closed, emergency veterinary clinics will not attend on site to help, where people cannot afford to own a car or drive to a veterinary centre or wildlife hospital, where the callers are too young to drive, or have phobias of birds and other creatures.

On one occasion we stopped to help a female driver whose car had hit a deer close to our rescue centre. The lady was on her own, crying and in shock. The deer was lying in the road and her car was badly damaged. We checked the deer which sadly died, and then sat with the lady for over 30 minutes till a relative came along. WRAS has also been called out by several people with bird phobias. On one occasion it was by a mother who was about to drive her daughter to school. However on finding an injured gull in their driveway they couldn't bring themselves to leave their house. When I arrived they were in floods of tears and a state of upset and fear. We removed the gull and took it into care, and mother and daughter were extremely grateful for our help, and having calmed down and been reassured, drove off to school. Having said that; WRAS will not, and legally cannot, remove healthy wildlife from gardens because, for whatever reason, residents do not want them there. We are not a pest control company.

Health and Safety is an important aspect in today's society and WRAS is no exception. We have rescuers who are trained to deal with a variety of casualties that could prove dangerous were members of the public to attempt to help them. When in pain wildlife such as badgers, foxes, seals, swans, geese, gannets, squirrels, deer and many other species can lash out, causing nasty bites that could potentially lead to bad infections. Badgers and seals in particular can cause the loss of use of a finger or tendon damage. Any such injury can result in the victim having to take time off work, and more often than not a trip to hospital. If a frightened deer stabs its antlers into your chest or kicks out with its leg, the outcome could easily be fatal if you are standing in the wrong place and unused to dealing with these animals. WRAS rescuers help members of the public avoid becoming sick or injured as a result of having to deal with a casualty because no one else will. Our rescuers are a valuable community service helping to keep members of the public safe.

Wildlife is part of our heritage, countryside and our parks and gardens. Tourists are drawn to these areas and nobody wants to see a badger that's been hit by a car dragging its back legs across a picnic area, a deer caught in stock fencing whilst taking a country walk, or an oil covered guillemot on the beach whilst sun bathing. Such events can ruin a holiday. WRAS can help ensure tourists still enjoy their holiday by providing assistance, ensuring they go away happy and satisfied that the casualty was rescued and given the best possible chance of surviving.

Another part of our work that benefits the community, and one that many might not know about, is the help WRAS gives to students from Plumpton College, Canterbury University and Hadlow College work experience. We give them work placements to help with their college courses, as well as various back-to-work schemes that enable unemployed people to gain new experiences and new skills. We have even registered with the Sussex Youth Offending Team to help those youngsters that have gone astray change their lives for the better. Let's not forget that we also have many volunteers who join us in order to gain experience, a focus and fulfil an ambition.

So East Sussex WRAS, is not just providing a Casualty Care Centre that helps wildlife, but also a valuable community service assisting the public on a daily basis.

On 29th April 2011, while most people were glued to their TVs watching the Royal Wedding of Prince Charles and Camilla, a group of ducklings were following their mum across the busy A22 at Eastbourne. Unfortunately the mother was run over and killed but the ducklings scattered across the road in panic. We received 7 calls from concerned motorists as rescuers rushed to the scene. By then the ducklings had hidden themselves in the grass verge or worse, among the bushes, brambles and nettles that bordered the road. After a good three hours of scouring the prickly undergrowth, we managed to catch twelve out of a possible fourteen ducklings. Despite hours of searching, the remaining two had disappeared.

By the time we had finished gathering up the little bundles of fluff we were scratched and stung to bits, but satisfied we had done the best we could. 'The Royal Family', as we had named them, were taken to the nearby Blackberry Farm Children's Activity Centre on the A22 where staff there reared them.

Several days later, on the 5th May, there was another duckling alert. Numerous worried motorists called us about a mother duck and her brood on the B2191 Hide Hollow, between Langney and Westham. Rescuers Tony and Les rushed to the rescue. Despite having been hit by a car, luckily this time mum was alive. Once again the ducklings had scattered, amazingly without any having been killed and rescuers again had the hard job of searching for them in the undergrowth. The mum was given treatment at St Anne's Vets in Eastbourne and then taken to WRAS's Casualty Care Centre for observation and placed in a large pen with her babies. After a long spell of treatment they were all successfully transported to a nearby stream and returned to the wild.

The centre was really taking off and between 2011 and 2014 our quiet periods seemed few and far between. The autumn weather was warmer than normal and summer seemed to last longer and go straight into winter without much of an autumn. This caused a number of problems for our wildlife which needs the autumn to prepare for hibernation or fattening up in order to survive the harsher weather of winter. Our busy spring and summer season is very expensive and we need the quieter times of year to recuperate funds so we can cope with the next busy season. This really caused WRAS problems to the point that several appeals had to be run in order to bring in vital funding to cope.

Kathy was now trying to manage over 60 volunteers. I was trying to co-ordinate 17 rescuers as part of a new on-call system and started to have rescuers based at the centre. We also now had volunteers coming in and helping to manage our new supporter database, helping to put newsletters, appeals and donation thank you letters together and packaging them up and posting them.

Over the next few years WRAS grew from strength to strength, but not without a few internal problems. I discovered that behind my back I was being bad-mouthed by a couple of volunteers, one after the other. On a number of occasions rumours were spread and I found myself getting very stressed and anxious again. Unfortunately there are those who hear one version of events and treat it as gospel without listening to or even considering that there is another side to the story. It's frustrating when someone builds your trust in them, you feel you can rely on them only to find they are taking advantage using your trust to their advantage and to turn people against you. They push and encourage people to moan and complain but would never do it themselves trying to stay favoured by those on both sides of a confrontation. Sadly these people eventually are their own downfall and I have had some stressful times having to deal with them.

One person who ended up leaving was so disgruntled they went on a hate campaign and complained to everyone they could think of about whatever they could dream up, even reporting to the Fire Service that we had locked Fire Escapes even though there were no locks on them! The whole process was very distressing, and I found it a very anxious time as we spent 8 months with various organisations contacting us after receiving complaints.

For a while I found myself getting very depressed about the whole situation and ended up having to seek counselling.

Having spoken to people in a number of other organisations I have discovered that I am not alone in encountering such negativity from people. It is one of the downsides of becoming successful. There are those, it seems, who are jealous of that success and want to fast track onto the back of it without working hard to achieve it.

I look back on this tormenting time, I am actually please it happened, as it has helped with WRAS's development. Having grown so much over the past 6 years and the workings of the charity has changed so much and the income increased that the old ways of working needed changing. WRAS had changed from just me working with the vets to look after casualties to there being a team of people and multiple vets. Policies and procedures needed writing, legalities needed confirming, paper work and forms needed developing and improving. The Royal College of Veterinary Surgeons have been very useful in helping to advice best practice and clarify certain legalities in what we do. There are limitations on what we can do as rehabbers and not as veterinary surgeons, and this balance can be difficult to get right. We are not hear to replace vets, but we have built up extensive knowledge on first aid, as well as what casualties can tolerate and cope with once released back to the wild. Veterinary support is vital for the sake of the animal's welfare. With all the best will in the world, I can't operate on a casualty and wouldn't dream of doing so. There are various emergency first aid procedure which we are allowed to undertake under the instruction of a veterinary surgeon, but WRAS only allows those trained by our vets to do so. Where for example I might tie off an arterial bleed as an emergency procedure to save an animal's life, it would have to be followed up as soon as possible afterwards by one of our veterinary surgeons checking what I had done and looking at a more long term solution. Under the Veterinary Surgeons Act only a vet can make a diagnosis, although it does get confusing sometimes between what is a diagnosis and what is an observation – I can observe the bone protruding from the leg of a fox and say it is fractured but after taking an X-ray I can't make a diagnosis of a fractured leg, this would have to be confirmed by a vet. Our vets have been valuable in supporting us with operations, amputations, sedation, diagnostic work, laboratory work and teaching us first aid and lifesaving principles to help the casualties we come across.

With the much need support of our volunteers, supporters and vets we were fortunate both the bad atmosphere and the rumour-mongering gradually dissipated and life at WRAS returned to normal. Well as normal as it ever can be when working with wild, and often unpredictable, creatures – be they animal or human.

Chapter 16 - Up Up and away!

On New Year's Day 2012 I received several phone calls from members of the public distressed to see a duck with a 5 inch dart through its neck swimming around the Pells Pond in Lewes. They were all very concerned and upset. When rescuers Tony, Claire and I arrived the male duck was still quite mobile and swimming around on the pond and we had to draft several members of the public to help catch him.

Four local residents joined us, including Lewes Town Council Ranger Chris Kemp. Tony, wearing a dry-suit, was already in the water, but it soon became clear that we weren't going to be able to catch the duck unless we jumped in too. The water was very cold, and in places more than waist deep; we knew we would not be able to stay in the water very long. It's a good job I'm not bothered about having children!

It took us five attempts to catch the duck before eventually local resident Jack Lee skilfully managed to catch him, trapping him in a net before the duck dived in an attempt to evade capture. Jack did a great job and without his help and that of all the local residents the duck would probably have suffered a slow and horrible death. The local residents and anglers present were extremely pleased that the duck had been rescued. It never fails to amaze me how concerned people are about wildlife.

The duck was taken back to our Casualty Care Centre, where the dart was cleaned and carefully removed and the wounds then cleaned and treated. There was a small infection which had set in as the dart had been in place for at least 24hours. Luckily it had only pierced the muscle at the back of the duck's neck, but just a centimetre lower and his fate could have been completely different.

After a couple of weeks of care the duck was ready for release and we returned him to the pond where he happily joined his fellow ducks.

2011 and 2012 proved to be a steep learning curve for Kathy. We had decided to take the plunge and start hand-rearing baby pigeons and doves ourselves. We asked Sam Bedford from Bedfordshire Wildlife Rescue if she would come over and pass on her vast expertise and knowledge which has been invaluable.

Kathy's first pigeon was little 'Rosie' a very feisty three week old Wood Pigeon. Rosie did not like being fed and her spirited attitude taught us a lot about handling young birds. After eight weeks she was big and strong enough to be successfully released. Kathy's next patients were some very poorly four week old feral pigeons, and then her first two Collared Doves. With far tinier beaks, they are so much more delicate looking than the pigeons and it was a great experience to rear them. Shortly after that we had a real challenge on our hands in the shape of 'Teasel and Thistle', two tiny bundles of fluff. They were one day old feral pigeon chicks found on the ground in a multi-storey car park and almost frozen to death. It was amazing to see them develop over the weeks, and incredible how they can change even overnight.

Although a few of our previous volunteers had hand-reared baby birds in small numbers, it was not till we set up our Casualty Centre that we were able to do so in a more professional way. The role is now shared; so less stressful and not reliant on just one person. There is a rota of dedicated people who start from as early as 6am and work right through till 11pm in shifts. How often each bird is fed depends on its species and age. Tiny baby birds can need feeding as often as every 15minutes. It's a bit like painting the Forth Bridge! Missing a feed, not mixing the food correctly or using the wrong moisture content can all prove fatal, so rearing orphans and knowing what to do when something goes wrong is crucial.

Kathy's biggest success that year was 'Godric' a two week old Wood Pigeon who came in unable to stand or balance. He sat with his legs sticking out in front of him and fell to one side if unsupported. He had very poor feather development with most of his flight feathers missing from his wings. Over a period of two weeks 'Godric' gained some strength and gradually began to bear his own weight, then taking a few wobbly steps, he managed to balance himself with his wings. Eventually he went into an aviary equipped with a 'climbing frame' that allowed him to grow stronger and achieve better balance. We still did not know if he would ever fly again but felt there was enough of a chance to try. In late autumn Godric finally moulted, his new flight feathers emerged and he began to fly clumsily at head height. He was then able to go into a larger aviary with other Woodies and they were all eventually released in the late autumn.

That summer Kathy had a new recruit to her rearing team, Kate who was a great help. Amongst others Kate looked after the terrible trio 'Starsky & Hutch' plus 'Kojak', three feral pigeon squeakers; a term we use to describe young pigeons older than chicks with feathers starting to come through. This threesome had supposedly been found in the same nest without parents, even though Kojak was a week younger.   Kate ended the year with a very late pair of feral babies, 'Snakes and Ladders'. These she had rescued from a nest in a tree about to be felled under licence. They were only five days old; one was white and the other grey. Carrie also joined the rearing team and expanded our ability to take in even more small birds. In all we reared over eighty baby doves and pigeons that year.

During the cold, snowy and icy weather in February I received over thirty calls over several days from concerned members of the public who mistakenly thought that a resident swan at the Pells Pond, Lewes, was stuck in the ice. The reasons they gave were many and various; "I can't see one of the swan's legs"; "It's been sitting in the same place as I saw it earlier; "It's on its last legs and dying"; "Its body is beneath the ice and therefore trapped within the ice" plus "Its neck is out-stretched and it's in a lot of discomfort and distress".   At one point I found myself and various colleagues rushing over to the Pells Pond three times in one day, only to find that the swan was not stuck and in good health.

We have no choice but to take these calls very seriously and to attend on site just in case anything has changed since our last visit. Swans do occasionally get stuck but it is quite uncommon. Every single visit we made to the pond, the swan turned out not to be stuck and in good health.

And yet, despite our many visits, people were still convinced that the swan was ice-bound. One day, having already checked on the swan twice, ten minutes after returning from my last visit, I received a call from a lady who said the swan was clearly trapped in the ice as its body was partially under the ice. Despite explaining that the entire pond had been iced over for at least three days and it was therefore impossible in the last ten minutes for this to have happened she insisted that the swan was definitely trapped and going to die if we didn't do something. So to relieve her anxiety and put her mind at rest once again we returned to the pond. Not surprisingly the swan was neither stuck nor under the water.

Swans fatten themselves up before winter knowing there will be times when food is limited; they also tuck their feet up under their soft, duvet-like feathers to keep warm. It is also warmer to sit on the ice than to swim in the freezing cold water. Swans will conserve energy during cold weather by not standing up or walking around much unless they have to. Their body temperature creates smooth patches around where they sit which can make it slippery when they try to stand, so they often prefer to stay right where they are till the cold snap passes.

While the Pells Pond iced-in-swan episode may sound as though it exasperated me, which to be honest it did a bit, as people just wouldn't take my word for it that the swan was not ice-bound but just resting and conserving her energy, it was encouraging to see so many people keeping an eye out for our wildlife. Following the New Year's Eve darted-duck alert, it was good to know that people were being very vigilant.

However, it was a relief when the warmer weather came and the calls stopped coming in.

In March 2012 we responded to an emergency call via the Badger Trust Sussex, after a demolition company reported what they thought were badger cubs squeaking underground where they were working. Staff showed us where the badgers were thought to be. Tony and I had to use our hands to scrabble away the broken concrete to get to the cubs. The entire den had collapsed around them. One of them was clearly dead; the other three were very cold and hypothermic. Tony and Claire slowly warmed them up but sadly and rather upsettingly another one of them died.

The remaining two were so cold it was impossible to try feeding or giving them water. Claire took over warming them up whilst Tony drove them up to Folly Wildlife Rescue near Tunbridge Wells. Annette and Dave, the local orphaned badger experts, took over their care.

The demolition company stopped all work on the site and were advised to contact Natural England before continuing. An Environmental survey of the site had been undertaken before the work was started but it clearly missed this badger sett that went under the foundations. We could not have asked the demolition company to have been more co-operative and helpful.

Annette, at Folly Wildlife Rescue, told us that the boy badger was feeding well and gaining weight nicely, but his sister was really struggling. She unfortunately died a week later and fortnight after that her brother, the last remaining cub, also sadly died. They certainly didn't have the best start in life, were extremely underweight for their age, approximately five weeks old when rescued with their eyes just opening. Annette tried her best, and if anyone could have saved them it would have been her.

A nursery school in Isfield phoned me in March 2012 after finding a gorgeous Tawny Owl caught up in chain link fencing on Rocks Park Road, in Uckfield. We think it probably had a close encounter with a passing car or lorry and was blown against the fence. Luckily the owl was just concussed and had a minor wound to his upper beak. I collected the owl from the nursery and took it back to our centre. After an assessment and treatment the owl was housed in one of WRAS' newly constructed indoor pens. After a few days in care, and showing that he could fly well in the pens, the owl was taken back and released in Rocks Park.

During the spring and autumn, when darkness falls around the same time as commuter traffic heads to and from work, we go through an increase in road casualties. Birds like owls will be hunting along grass verges during dusk and dawn looking for food. While they concentrate on looking for little creatures to catch they don't notice the traffic. This results in WRAS being called out to pick up the pieces, or at least those birds that are not literally in pieces, but are stunned, disorientated or injured.

One piece of equipment donated in the summer of 2012 was a new Ultrasound machine for our first aid room. Vet Simon Harris, used the machine to check a road casualty Badger in WRAS' care which was

161

suspected of having a ruptured abdominal wall. The machine was also used to check the bladder and other organs for internal damage and for pregnancies in hedgehogs. We decided to make a start on developing our own x -ray room.

WRAS always gets an influx of pheasant casualties during the winter when thousands are released for so called countryside sports. In order to escape the hunting and shooting, many pheasants are starting to move into towns. Quite a few of them seem attracted to the seafronts at Hove and Eastbourne.

A more usual spot for them though, is inland in the countryside. So it was with that I attended an unusual call from Lewes Railway Station. They needed assistance with a pheasant. A train driver had picked up the bird just outside Falmer on the edge of the Downs, and handed it to staff at Lewes on his arrival. I drove over to Lewes to collect the pheasant from the Station Master's Office. It was unable to stand but was not paralysed. Unfortunately, after a few weeks of care, the vet decided her legs were not going to recover and sadly she had to be put down.

In May 2012 I received a letter from the Cabinet Office saying "The Prime Minister has asked me to inform you, that having accepted the advice of the Head of the Civil Service and the Main Honours Committee, he proposes to submit your name to the Queen. He is recommending that Her Majesty may be graciously pleased to approve that you be appointed a Member of the Order of the British Empire (MBE) in the Birthday 2012 Honours List."

I opened the letter whilst in a long queue of traffic on my way to the Casualty Centre one morning. I had to pull over into a lay-by to re-read it several times. To say the least, I was shocked and in tears. I never thought I would ever be proposed for anything like this. I felt privileged to be named for such a prestigious award.

The letter explains that you are not to tell anyone and keep it strictly confidential. As the weeks went on and I didn't hear anything more, I started to feel this was someone having a laugh. I spoke to Alan Knight, of International Animal Rescue, who had been awarded an OBE a few years previously, asking him what communication he had received and what had happened. He told me that he had felt exactly the same way when his letter dropped on his mat.

Final confirmation came on 16th June when the Honours List was published in the London Gazette and some national newspapers. I now had to wait for an invitation to an Investiture organised by the Central Chancery of the Order of Knighthood, based at St James's Palace.

Although this honour was awarded to me I would like to express my personal thanks to all our loyal volunteers and supporters without whom neither I nor WRAS would exist and my role helping wildlife would not be possible. I do not see

this award as being mine, but as a national acknowledgement of everyone past and present that has helped make me and WRAS who we are, and made my involvement in WRAS what it is today.

I feel deeply honoured to receive this award, and I hope this will help bring in funding and prove our commitment to helping wildlife in need.

Three days later I was rushing to Newhaven Harbour after a report of a fox trapped in a barge on the River Ouse. We attended using two ambulances.

We had to use our ladders to get down to the bottom of the barge, about 20ft deep. Initially we were perplexed. The fox had disappeared. After a bit of a search, eventually we found him hiding between two large twenty metre long metal girders. He was going to be extremely difficult to reach.

We tried strapping some poles together to try and push the fox out but these broke, so I drove to the local plumbing supplies company and bought two sets of drainage rods to see if that would work.

We positioned ourselves at suitable locations in order to catch the fox once it came out. After a bit of poking and probing with the rods, the fox came out and Tony managed to grab it with the catch net and put it in the waiting cage. At first we thought the fox might have been injured but on closer inspection it was obviously fine. We then had the difficult job of getting the fox up the ladder and out of the barge. As we pushed the cage up the ladder the fox could sense he was being removed from the barge and became more active. It was quite a tricky climb; 20ft up a ladder holding a cage containing a frisky fox.

Back at WRAS's Casualty Care Centre, we checked him over and confirmed that he wasn't injured, except for a small graze to the mouth where he had tried to bite the catch net. The fox was given the all clear and taken back late that night for release. We obviously couldn't release him in the barge, so we liberated him nearby at the old and now disused Newhaven Marina Station.

The arrival of summer brought with it a series of amusing rescues. At least they made us laugh!

Having released quite a few casualties back to the wild over the previous few weeks, we decided to go shopping for more casualties. With funds tight and trying to keep costs down and looking for a bargain we visited Poundland. Only joking!

Poundland had called us out after a young wood pigeon had decided to walk in through the front doors. The young bird, frightened by a shopper, had flown up to the top of a shelving unit, then fallen down behind it and become stuck. I wonder if he'd been looking for the bird food section.

Using a ladder and torch I peered down the back of the wall unit and saw the pigeon right at the bottom at floor level, clearly stuck between the shelving unit and the wall of the store. I was really unsure of how we were going to get to the bird as the staff at the store did not think it was possible to get behind the unit from the bottom.

Kathy and I cleared the sweets from a section of the shelving, removed the shelves and luckily found a metal plate that the staff were then able to unscrew. This left a 2.5 inch gap under the shelving and we were just about able to get our fingers under to hold the pigeon and slowly and carefully manoeuvre it out. We checked him over and discovered he had a minor wound to one leg so we gave him some medication and took him back to be bedded down at the centre. We told the pigeon he should have gone to Specsavers!

In August 2012 I contacted the press asking for their help in encouraging the public to dispose of potentially dangerous fat-ball feeders before they caused harm to wildlife.

On three occasions I had been called out to rescue starlings that had been caught inside fat-ball feeders. We urged people to check their fat-ball feeders and to dispose of them if their lids were missing. The three rescued starlings had all been found trapped inside feeders, trying to reach the last bits of the fat-balls. These situations are very stressful for the birds and some will injure themselves before we get a chance to rescue them. Prevention is always better than cure. So if you have a fat-ball feeder, which is a good thing, put this book down and please go outside and check that the feeder isn't missing a lid, which is a bad thing and can endanger the birds you are trying to help. It doesn't take a moment to ensure your fat-balls are safe.

Most feeders are generally ok to use, but it is important to ensure they are in good working order and not hazardous. Another problem we occasionally see is birds' legs caught in the netting bags left over from fat balls that have been hung in trees and bushes. So if you put out fat balls, do remember to remove them from the netting bags or buy ones without the netting.

At 8.45pm one weekend evening we were called to the aid of a swan which was trapped on a bridge above the river Adur at Shoreham. Concerned residents had been unable to find any local organisations able to attend as they don't have the resources to do out of hours rescues, so WRAS stepped in. The swan was thought to have crash landed on the footbridge which crosses between Shoreham Beach and Shoreham Town Centre. To make matters worse the bridge was currently closed off with high security fencing.

When we arrived two local residents were talking to the swan, feeding it bread and trying to keep it close to the end of the footbridge so it would be easier for us to catch. But with a seven foot high security fence between us and the swan, it was not going to be that simple.

In order to scale the fence we climbed up the concrete pillars and the original bridge railings. It was by no means easy to get over and I managed to rip the back of my trousers in the process!

With one buttock cheekily peeping out through the tear, I cornered the swan, checked it over and then passed the 10kg bird up to my ever understanding girlfriend Kathy; perched gracefully on the top of the concrete pillar. Kathy then held onto the swan while I clambered rather ungracefully back over the security fencing.

Safely back on the road side we carried the swan across the marshland towards the river. As it was by now very dark, we took it as far as we safely could, before releasing it and letting it waddle off back to its rightful place on the river.

I suspect the swan had probably collided with the bridge in the dark and landed by chance on the footbridge. The local residents told us it had been walking backwards and forwards for well over an hour before they decided it needed help. Had we not come to the rescue it would have been stuck there till the morning and potentially been attacked by a fox or dog. It was good to see him released and we were glad he didn't have any injuries. The only damage done was to my trousers - and my dignity.

Chapter 17 - Life has its ups and downs!

Night time calls are not that common but, like buses, you get none for ages then they all come along at once. The busiest times for calls are the spring and autumn. Just after 11pm on Monday 15th October 2012 I was called out to Ridgewood in Uckfield after a gentleman phoned me about a badly injured wood pigeon. I had already gone to bed but as it was local to me, I got up and jumped in my ambulance. The pigeon wasn't as bad as I had expected so drove it to our centre, treated it and bedded it down. On my way home I turned off the A22 onto Eastbourne Road, Uckfield, when a car overtook me and pulled in front of me with hazard lights on. Having been stopped in similar ways on previous occasions I assumed that the person had a casualty or wanted to tell me about one he had seen. I got out of the ambulance to see what the problem was and before I knew what was happening, the man grabbed my throat, forcefully pinned me to the side of the ambulance and started demanding, "Where are the drugs. Give me your drugs!".

I desperately tried to keep the situation calm and not to escalate or antagonise him. I kept saying "We are not vets, we're a charity we don't carry drugs on board". After what seemed like ages, the man was clearly getting frustrated and gave up, shoving my head and neck back hard against the ambulance before running to his car and driving off at speed.

I called Sussex Police to report the incident and two officers arrived who took a full statement whilst the details were still fresh in my mind. My partner Kathy had also driven over and took me home. I really kicked myself afterwards as I didn't even think to look at the registration number of the attacker's car, as I was so shocked.

But I could remember what he looked like. It's an image that will stay with me for quite a long time. He was white, probably in his early 30s and about 6ft tall with short dark coloured hair and stubble on his face. His car was a dark coloured, old style, either Ford or Vauxhall hatchback .

I called a meeting of our rescuers to discuss night time work and to seriously consider whether we should continue to do it. However, everyone agreed that we had to; that we shouldn't let one isolated incident put us off, no matter how unpleasant and threatening this had been. But we all agreed that we should start reporting in what we were doing and where we were going so that no-one was ever out on a rescue without somebody else knowing about it.

I was too shocked to go to work the following day and volunteers Kate, Jayden, Tony and Dave all helped cover and take control for the day, which was very much appreciated. For the next few months I found myself getting nervous about what other cars were doing and locking my vehicle doors. I would also like to thank Sussex Police for their support.

WRAS ambulances are not stocked with medication although we do have an emergency medication bag which is taken out on some rescues. It is not stored in the vehicles and we don't keep controlled drugs like Ketamine, which is what my attacker was probably after. The main ambulances now have an inexpensive CCTV installed for safety.

After the official announcement that I was being awarded an MBE, I received several letters and phone calls from people asking me to turn down the honour as a protest against the Royal Family's stance on hunting. For years I had thought the same; that I wouldn't accept such an honour. I spoke to Alan Knight about this and why he had accepted his honour. Alan explained that the honours are not decided by the Royal Family but by a committee made up of various dignitaries within various government offices. Members of the public submit nominees they feel worthy of an honour, and the committee then consider the application forms. If they come to the conclusion that you have done enough to warrant an honour they then write to inform you.

I came to the conclusion that turning down the honour would not have any effect on the Royal Family and their hunting activities. To refuse would also be one hell of a kick in the teeth to those people who had submitted my name for such a national honour. So I decided to accept.

On 24th October I travelled to London where I met my father and step-mum who very generously paid for Kathy and me to stay overnight in the very posh, four star 'Rubens at the Palace Hotel', before going to the Palace for my investiture.

It was an amazing experience, and I felt very out of place, but the palace staff were light hearted and calm, they had everything in order and well planned and everything ran on well-oiled wheels. I was one of the last batches of people to be shown through to receive my award. We were told how to approach, to wait for your surname to be read out, then to walk forward, turn, bow, and finally approach Prince Charles. He asked me where I came from, how long had I been doing animal rescue, and said he was pleased that my work had been noticed and that I was receiving the award. It seemed to pass very quickly.

I am glad I have proved so many people wrong about where I was going with my life and voluntary work. I might be poor but I am so much happier as a result. I'm glad I am achieving something with my life. I am sad that my mum is not alive to have witnessed this and been able to accompany me to the Palace. I hope that she would have been proud of me, although she would have panicked about what to wear.

After the investiture we meet up with Stephen Lloyd, MP for Eastbourne, and I am very grateful for him to take time out of his busy schedule to meet us. WRAS does more work in his constituency than any other and he has always been very supportive of our work, even before he became an MP.

I must reiterate that the work we do within WRAS would not be possible if it was not for the volunteers and the supporters of our charity. They are the backbone of WRAS and without their dedicated support it would not be possible for us to rescue the volume of animals we care for.

It was good to get away for a couple of days, but within 24 hours of my return I was back in my work gear and getting mucky again!

I believe that if I can be given such an honour then there are hundreds of people currently working in this field that deserve it way more than I do. I hope more of those helping animals are nominated for such awards. Perhaps that way we will have a bigger impact on whether people undertake blood sports or not.

One month later, to my amazement, I was contacted by BBC Radio Sussex who told me that I had been nominated for their first ever Community Heroes Award for Animal Welfare.

I was invited to their awards' evening at Wakehurst Place, Ardingly, on Thursday 13th December 2012. I was up against two other people and not all sure whether

or not I would be successful amongst so many other deserving people. Virginia McKenna OBE, an amazing woman, had been invited to announce the winner and present the award. I couldn't believe it when she read out my name. I was astonished and delighted.

For those not old enough to remember, Virginia McKenna is perhaps best remembered for her 1966 role as Joy Adamson in the true-life film, "Born Free" for which she received a nomination for a Golden Globe. Bill Travers, her real life husband, co-starred with her, portraying conservationist George Adamson. The experience led them to become active supporters for wild animal rights and the protection of their natural habitat. Virginia McKenna also appeared in "An Elephant Called Slowly", a travelogue of what it was like years ago in Kenya. The film features her close friend conservationist George Adamson and also elephants "Eleanor" (brought up by conservationist Daphne Sheldrick) and young "Pole Pole" (Swahili "Slowly Slowly"). The subsequent premature death of Pole Pole in London Zoo lead to Virginia and her husband launching the Zoo Check Campaign in 1984 and to establishing the "Born Free Foundation" in 1991.

Virginia gave an inspiring speech saying, "I have found this evening a most inspirational occasion. We are absolutely bombarded with bad news, sad news, shocking news and in this room tonight, is nothing but hope and positive thought".

There are millions of wild animals every year who have to be euthanized because there just aren't enough wildlife organisation capable of dealing with the workload of sick, injured and orphaned wildlife. East Sussex is luckier than most counties having organisations like Rogers Wildlife Rescue, Folly Wildlife Rescue, Kit Wilson Trust, WRAS and the RSPCA centre at Hastings who are able to take in wildlife, but it still isn't enough. There is a chronic shortage of funds available for this type of work in the UK. I am so pleased that BBC Radio Sussex and Surrey have seen the need to have a dedicated award for Animal Welfare and to be the first person to receive it.

Rescue work and animals getting injured doesn't stop just because there is an awards ceremony taking place. During the evening I had to juggle between listening to speeches and answering our rescue phone line. The latter half of the evening saw two road casualty owls and a fox in need of help, to which our ambulances and rescuers swiftly responded.

The beginning of 2013 saw us urging people to "Think Hedgehog" after a hedgehog was impaled on a garden fork. It had been found in a garden near Northiam, whilst landscaping and garden clearance was taking place, and was extremely lucky to be alive. Unfortunately, the finder had kept it in a shed for two days, not knowing what to do with it. The longer an injured animal is kept untreated, the smaller its chances of survival become. So while you might think you are helping an animal by keeping it safe, the better course of action is to alert WRAS as soon as possible.

It was rushed by ambulance to our casualty centre. One of the wounds was quite smelly and infected and the second was not so bad, but both clearly quite deep. I was expecting much worse. Quite often the puncture wounds are central on the body and can result in horrendous internal injuries, often fatal. In this case very luckily the fork had speared either side of the hedgehog's main body cavity avoiding the vital areas.

The hedgehog was seen by our vet and the wounds cleaned using a warm diluted iodine bath. He was placed on antibiotics and amazingly made a complete recovery.

We issued a press release asking gardeners to "Think Hedgehog" whilst clearing gardens and to be careful of locations where hedgehogs might be hibernating.

Hedgehogs hibernate in all sorts of locations; including under and inside sheds, in greenhouses, in pampas grass, compost heaps, and thick vegetation using grass and leaves. We have even found then in piles of rubble, under decking surrounded by plastic bags and litter, and some have

171

been partially buried in soil and leaves under bushes. So be careful when clearing areas, a hibernating hedgehog will not always be where you might expect.

If you do ever disturb a nesting hedgehog, the best advice is to place it back and cover it exactly as you found it. Once disturbed, they will often go and find a new place to stay, but if they don't, or if the nest is too badly destroyed or the hedgehog is injured in anyway, then seek advice and call your local rescue centre for help straight away.

In March 2013 motorists were oblivious to a major rescue taking place about 50 metres off Uckfield High Street. Two of our veterinary ambulances from Uckfield and Polegate were responding to a call about a female roe deer which had been spotted by local residents running between gardens in Bedford Court just off Uckfield High Street. This potentially posed a real risk to unsuspecting traffic in the busy high street just after morning rush hour.

We had also received calls from several motorists who had previously seen her running up the High Street and past their cars. Luckily she didn't stop at the Butchers!

When we arrived at first we couldn't find the deer. After a search of the area we found her hiding behind a row of garages. In situations like this we would normally leave the animal alone and allow it to sort itself out. But being in such a busy area and so close to the High Street, there was a real risk to people and traffic, and the last thing we wanted was the deer to cause an accident and potentially get herself killed in the process.

We used ladders to climb over a wall and fence so two rescuers could position themselves on either side of the deer. Whilst our hearts were racing, motorists only about 50 metres away from us had no idea what was going on. You have to be so careful with deer, they are extremely sensitive and also very powerful animals. We were reluctant to use sedatives as this would cause delays in any release and potentially be more stressful to the deer. It took four of us to gain control of the deer which we pinned on either side using stretchers as safety barriers. We then covered her with blankets and once we were in full control we lifted her in a rather un-ladylike fashion to the waiting ambulance where she was placed on her

172

keel; i.e. upright on her chest, with two rescuers accompanying her. The ambulance drove the short distance to the Sussex Horse Rescue Trust's land at the end of Hempstead Lane in Uckfield, where the deer was then released into a field. It was a bit of a struggle getting her out of the ambulance and over the fence, but once down on the ground and after taking a few seconds to compose herself she was up and off. We monitored her as she ran across the field, negotiated several fences and ditches and away. It was clear she knew the area because rather than panicking about how to navigate the fences and ditches she went straight to the crossing points with ease. She definitely knew where she was. It was one of two likely areas where I thought she might have come from; fortunately I'd got the right one.

Planning often takes longer than the actual rescues in these situations. We have to ensure we know what we are doing and avoid any unnecessary delays. Capture to release took less than 20 minutes and this is important for the deer's welfare.

In April we were approached by a television production company to say we had been nominated for a new television animal award; The British Animal Honours 2013. This was a brand new ITV event celebrating the achievements of the country's most extraordinary animals and the people who work with them. To our surprise East Sussex WRAS had been nominated for the Local Animal Charity of the Year Award.

The programme was to be filmed in front of a live audience and hosted by Paul O'Grady, and was inspired by the UK's unwavering connection with animals. In a press release Paul O'Grady said, "Animals protect us in war zones, keep our borders safe and allow the disabled to live independently. Some give us national glory in sporting events while others are the showbiz scene-stealers that make us laugh and cry in movies, on TV and online."

After the other recent awards we couldn't believe it when we were again nominated. It certainly sounded as though it would be an amazing evening. More than anything I was pleased that the award did not just recognise me but the work of the charity as a whole.

The past few years had been tough on our finances and seen an increase in casualty numbers. To ensure we can continue helping as many casualties as possible we have had to become even more cost effective than we were. As a result our volunteers and donors have been brilliant at supporting us and helping us to move onwards and upwards so that we can win such awards.

We were all so touched that people had nominated us for this award. When you look at how many individuals and organisations there are across the country, and the amazing work they do, I am really surprised that we made it onto the shortlist.

They sent a TV crew down to film a short clip of our work and we re-enacted part of a deer rescue from the previous year. This was so that they could use the actual rescue footage we had filmed at the time. Then it was back to normal at WRAS while we waited to see whether or not we had won.

April saw us called out to help two baby badgers that had been attacked by a dog at a field edge in Seaford. Kathy, Murrae and I searched the area but couldn't see them anywhere. The caller came out and met us and explained that whilst walking round the field two young badger cubs had come running up to him not seeming the least bit frightened. He had ignored them and kept walking but unfortunately a dog walker then entered the field. Their dog attacked the badgers and the owners had difficulty controlling it. The young badgers eventually ran off back to their sett in the hedgerow.

At the sett we saw the two young badgers very warily peeping out of their hole, they looked underweight, dehydrated and suffering from skin problems. Kathy had to be very patient in trying to coax them out.

Kathy slowly had to build up their confidence so they would come far enough out of their hole so she could catch them. Of course once the first one was caught the second became wary again.

The rescue took over an hour trying to catch both badgers one at a time, but eventually Kathy had both of them secured.

They were checked over, loaded into the ambulance and taken to Folly Wildlife Rescue near Tunbridge Wells to join another badger cub rescued earlier in the week.

Soon afterwards we were invited up to the BBC Elstree Studios in north London for the filming of the British Animal Honours Awards. Kathy, Kate and Lindsay and I attended representing WRAS and several of our volunteers managed to get tickets for the audience, which we were pleased about.

We got there mid-afternoon, and were taken to a waiting area before being shown to the studios. We were so excited and unsure what was going to happen, that food was the last thought on our minds. By the end of the evening we were all very hungry and thirsty as there were no drinks allowed in the studio.

They filmed the awards as if they were live with the occasional stop-start to ensure camera angles and introductions were correct. We were entertained by a wonderful performance of the stage production of "War Horse".

Eventually it came round the announcement of the winner of the award that we had been short-listed for. They showed the stag-rescue video that they had recently filmed. Then ITV 1 presenter Kate Garraway read the winner. It was us! Kathy, Kate, Lindsay and I went up on stage to receive the award and to talk to Kate Garraway and Paul O'Grady.

Yet again we were amazed to receive this national award. To be chosen as the local animal charity of the year when there are thousands of domestic, agricultural, and wildlife organisations around the country, is almost unbelievable. We clearly must be doing something right, and if I didn't have the trophies to prove it, I sometimes think they might all have been a dream.

I know I keep saying this, but although people tend to focus on me, WRAS would not exist without all our hardworking volunteers and the funding provided by our fantastic supporters. This award means more to me than the MBE I received last year because it is for the charity as a whole and is

175

recognition that our volunteers and supporters are a fabulous bunch of people who genuinely care about our local wildlife.

I promised that I would use these awards to help develop and promote the work of our charity and help us expand and grow for the sake of the wildlife casualties that desperately need our help.

In mid-May WRAS received a call about a seal on the beach just east of Sovereign Harbour, Eastbourne. I contacted BDMLR, reported the call and then attended on site with Stephen Marsh the Operations Director from BDMLR. We were surprised to find a large Grey Seal which looked fit and healthy. It was not that bothered about us. People were sitting on the beach only a matter of six feet away from it. As we approached it lifted its head and when we got too close it opened its mouth in defence and warned us off. Its body condition seemed fine and we took numerous photos and sent them to one of BDMLR's specialist vets for advice. We decided to back off and to keep dogs away from it. We called out a rota of Marine Mammal Medics, most of whom were WRAS volunteers anyway, to watch over the seal and keep him safe. Overnight the seal disappeared back into the water.

The following day the seal was discovered on Eastbourne Beach close to the Wish Tower, then later on near Holywell. A couple of days later the seal turned up on Seaford beach.

It is unusual for a grey seal to be seen on the East Sussex coast line. The nearest colonies are near Dover and on the North French coast. The stormy weather the two days before his arrival may have been the cause of him ending up here. Due to trouble on the first night it was decided that a watch was needed to keep him safe. A group of school children came down to the beach to see him and they decided to name him "Trevor". I'm not sure whether to be pleased or to go on a diet!

He spent six days on the beach at Seaford, occasionally going out to sea and then returning a few hours later. The first night at Seaford, medics ended up calling out police as youths tried to throw stones and dazzle the seal using laser pens. Medics also had problems with members of the public wanting to sit next to him to have their photo taken.

In the end we contacted Trevor Cutler at the Coastguard's office and asked for assistance. They came out with stakes and barrier tape to cordon off a safety area to keep people away from the seal.

We set up a round the clock watch and I took the night time shift from about 9pm through to 8am. At the beginning of the evening I would sit in the van or if there were people around I would stand by the cordon. In the early hours I would sleep in the ambulance but get up every half an hour to check he was ok. If anyone came along I would then get up to monitor the situation. At about 6am people would start arriving on the beach so I would get up and keep an eye on the situation.

Eventually it was clear that the seal was actually moulting and losing its winter coat. When this happens, like some other wild animals and birds, they feel very run down and lethargic. Seals normally haul out of the water in small groups to moult but don't normally do this on such public locations. Unlike dolphins, seals do not need to be in water and are happy to sun bathe on beaches.   Eventually he decided to move off and was seen in Brighton and Shoreham harbours and then seemed to move all the way down to Selsey Bill where he stayed for quite a few months.

I was called out to two hedgehogs at Westham in July 2013. They had to be the muddiest hedgehogs I have ever seen. They were found at the bottom of a very deep foundation trench on a building site. Builders discovered the pair, later named "Bill and Ben", and rescued them from the trench on their return to work on the Monday morning. The hedgehogs must have been stranded all weekend. I have never had to rescue hedgehogs as mud-caked as these. While we often find them with mud on, never before had we found them with so much caked and dried onto their fur and spines, especially round their faces.

We would normally release the hedgehogs back to their home range the same evening, but due to the on-going building work and the depth of the trench, we decided to keep the hedgehogs in care for a week until the trenches had been filled in. The first thing we did was to check to see if they were boys or girls, as we wouldn't want to keep a female away from her babies at this time of year. Luckily they were boys. Work experience student Bryony helped me wash them. You have to be careful when washing hedgehogs that they don't curl up and drown in the water.

After their bath, I don't think their spines had ever looked so clean. They were dried off and the two boys were bedded down for their stay awaiting their release.

The builders kept an eye on the trenches throughout the week and luckily no more hedgehogs became stuck. The following Monday they contacted us to say the trenches had been filled in, the concrete dried, and it was safe to release the hedgehogs.

We had a delightful call after a mother duck and her eleven ducklings were seen waddling around in the middle of a housing estate. Local residents of Birch Way, Hailsham, called us out at about 9:30am after spotting the family wandering in the road and were concerned that they might get run over. They had managed to encourage the itinerant duck family into their garden and confined them until our rescuers arrived.

Ducks frequently lay their eggs in gardens and parks as it is safer than nesting by a pond where all sorts of predators see both eggs and newly hatched ducklings as a tasty meal; gulls, mink, cats, foxes, birds of prey, corvids, pike, terrapins and many others are all expectantly licking their lips, so the mother finds a nice quiet garden where they are less likely to be found. Here she can nest in peace and quiet without even being pestered by male ducks.

Mother duck will normally know the route she wants to take back to her chosen pond but, as her ducklings are so young and can't fly, she has to walk them and this can cause them to get into trouble; falling down drains or getting run over.

When we checked the maps it was clear that there were several ponds which the mum and ducklings might head for, so rather than running the risk of catching them and mum flying off and abandoning them, or taking the ducks and releasing them at the wrong location, instead we decided to give them an escort.

With two rescuers behind and two in front, to prevent them from heading across drains, we also had a fifth person in an ambulance with flashing beacons who warned approaching traffic. The escort process took about twenty minutes to move from the garden and across the housing estate. Everyone was very helpful and happy to pass by our duck parade very carefully. The rescuers kept their distance so mum didn't feel threatened and felt comfortable to walk in her chosen direction. The whole family arrived safe and sound at her pond, a very satisfying outcome.

Although this duckling parade from garden to pond is quite a common occurrence, sadly these journeys often end in disaster with mum and youngsters being run over and killed. In other instances it is tempting to catch and move them, but if you release them on the wrong pond, the mother duck will only try to move them again to her chosen pond, without an escort, which can result in death and disaster on the busy roads.

At approximately 1am on the morning of Thursday 4th July 2013, I was in bed and asleep when the phone rang. There was a deer on the Uckfield railway line about 20-30 metres away from the Hempstead Lane crossing at Uckfield. A late night dog walker had spotted a male roe deer that seemed to have baler twine caught round its antlers and neck.

As I lived just a stone's throw away, I scrambled out of bed, got dressed, into the ambulance and arrived within fifteen minutes. I could see that the deer was clearly caught, but it was difficult to tell exactly how. My first concern was, "Is a train due"? I used the phone at the crossing to contact the Signal Box at Oxted. They advised that no trains were due.

At first it looked as though the baler twine was attached to a piece of wood, but on closer inspection I could see that the twine was also caught on part of the track fixings. The deer was stressed and exhausted, and it was clear that he had to be freed as soon as possible if he was going to stand any chance of surviving. As I approached to get a better look in the dark the deer flipped over and I took the rather risky opportunity to jump on it and pin it to the floor. Within just a few minutes I was able to cut the deer free and remove the twine that luckily was not tightly attached round the deer's neck.

179

To my delight the deer ran off through the bushes and away into the darkness and freedom. It was a good job the dog walker had spotted the deer and reported it when he did, otherwise it most likely would have died of stress by the morning or even been hit by an early train.

Kathy wasn't best pleased that I had tackled the deer on my own with no back up. She was right, of course, but the chance was there and I took it, making the rescue so much quicker and easier for the deer.

Chapter 18 - Nowt as queer as folk and wildlife!

2013 was a bizarre year with some odd rescues. Staff at Willingdon Primary School called us out having discovered a fox tangled up three feet off the ground in the middle of a bramble bush on their school playing field.

Rescuer Dave and I drove over and our ambulance was shown through the school and onto the playing field, where the school had cornered off the area to keep children away.

At first it was a bit of a mystery as to how the fox was caught up and dangling three feet from the ground. It quickly became apparent the fox had become entangled in a chain link fence behind the brambles, and was hanging by its rear leg. We cut a section of brambles away to get a closer look and used a dog grasper to support the front of the fox in case he fell. It was not easy to support the fox, and at the same time figure out exactly how the fox was attached, while working inside the middle of a thicket of brambles. I also had to take care I wasn't bitten by the fox in the process, so shielded myself as best I could using a large thick blanket.

Eventually I manage to cut the fox free and bring it down to ground level, but not without having incurred multiple scratches to my arms and face. We have dealt with various animals that have had their rear legs caught up in fencing but this was a first to find an animal caught just by one toe.

We rushed the fox back to our Casualty Care Centre where the wounds were cleaned and treated before being assessed and checked by our vet Chris. The fox had a fractured toe, several small wounds around the foot, and two open wounds on either side of the pelvis. This fox had been extremely lucky; it had been spotted early enough so that flies had only just started laying eggs on the wounds and there were no signs of maggots, and with the school summer holidays starting that day, the fox may not have been noticed at all and could have died a slow and horrible death.

After a small operation on the fox's foot, he was bedded down in one of our indoor pens. The pen had recently housed some owls and there was still a large trunk slung horizontally across the top of the pen about seven feet off the ground. Once the fox had begun to recover, a favourite trick was to jump off the side of

the pen, climb onto the branch and lie along it. When the volunteers opened the pen door to feed and clean the fox, they would get the shock of their lives; there was no fox to be seen on the floor of the cage – there he was peering down on them from his perch on the tree trunk.

After about six weeks of treatment the fox was suitable for release and taken back to his home in the school grounds. We hoped he'd learnt his lesson and would be a bit more careful in future.

Only a few weeks later we had another call out to a fox. John Bond, a volunteer at the Seaford Martello Tower Museum had discovered a fox inside the museum. The popular old Martello Tower Museum on Seaford's seafront has seen many visitors over the years, but as far as I know never before a curious fox.

The museum is surrounded by a moat and it was likely that fox may have jumped into the moat and been unable to get out again as the walls were too high. So he had probably hidden somewhere until a door was opened allowing him to get into the museum.

John had managed to corner the fox behind an old organ.

I went over with new rescuer Robert and we were led down the circular stairs into the depths of the museum. Foxes can get themselves into all sorts of odd locations and we've rescued them from roof tops, cellars, wall cavities, drains, and shop ceilings, but never before from a museum. This was a first for me.

The volunteers at the museum had done a great job in cornering the fox behind an old organ. Boxes and boards had been placed at either side of the organ to keep the fox contained. Using a dog grasper I tried to secure the fox. It took numerous attempts as the fox was a very lively fellow and kept biting the grasper preventing me from getting it over the fox's head. It took about fifteen minutes before I finally managed to secure the fox which we then placed on a blanket and checked him over.

He turned out to be a juvenile dog fox born earlier that year, and he didn't appear to be any the worse for wear through his visit to the museum. We placed him in a secure cage and carried him up the stairs and out to the waiting ambulance. It was a beautiful sunny day and the beach and seafront were very busy so obviously we couldn't just release the fox outside so we drove him back to our Casualty Care Centre and gave him food and water. That night Kathy and I returned and released the fox in the playing field next door to the museum.

We are often asked why we return foxes and other animals to where they came from, but they need to be in their home range, where they know the food sources and places of safety. Relocating any wild animal or bird and dumping it in an area it doesn't know would be an offence under the Abandonment of Animals Act.

Another unusual call was from staff at the Laughing Fish Pub, at Isfield. This time the casualty was a baby hedgehog. The caller reported finding a small hedgehog with something stuck to its back and clearly causing it distress.

At first sight it looked as though it was a crab apple or something similar that had stuck to the hedgehog's spines, but on closer inspection you could see that it was plastic and firmly attached. Kathy and I soon realised that the object was a Christmas bauble with a hanging loop for attaching to Christmas trees, and this loop was caught tightly around her body.

The loop went across her back and under her belly and had become embedded in her skin through various scabs and wounds. You could smell the infection. The hedgehog must have got her head and left leg through the loop when she was much smaller, and as she had grown the loop had become tighter and tighter. Had it remained in place, it would have eventually killed the baby hedgehog, so she was extremely lucky to have been found and saved thanks to the observant staff at the pub.

We rushed the 186 gram hedgehog to Henley House Vets in Uckfield where Veterinary Nurse Jenny and Vet Chris attended to her. She was given a general anaesthetic so that her wounds could be thoroughly cleaned and treated. I have never before seen such an unusual cause of a ligature wound and pressure necrosis on a wild animal. We have seen similar wounds caused by elastic bands, snares and netting, never before by a Christmas bauble.

We named the hedgehog "Izzy", having found at Isfield, and admitted her into care. She was an unusual case and had to return to the vets four times for her wounds to be cleaned up under anaesthetic. After about six weeks of care she made a good recovery and her wounds healed well. However by the end of October she was not big enough to be released before Winter. Generally hedgehogs need to be at least 600grams to safely survive hibernation, but Izzy was short of this so we took the decision to overwinter her in warmer conditions so she would remain awake, eating and drinking and putting on weight.

She was an unusual case because, out of the blue and without even being moved to a colder environment, she decided to hibernate. Spending weeks asleep and hardly eating anything her weight slowly reduced, just as a hibernating hedgehog's would.

Every now and then we do get the occasional hedgehog which despite being in a warm environment will still attempt to hibernate. More usually they will remain awake all winter, eating and drinking, when kept in this environment. We would never encourage a hedgehog to hibernate until they weigh more than 700grams and have finished treatment.

Izzy began to worry us when her weight dropped to just over 400 grams. We tried to warm her up to bring her out of hibernation, but she still continued to hibernate. Then one day out of the blue she woke up, started eating all her food and putting on weight again. We did faecal analysis on her to check all was well, and then moved her to an outside pen to ensure she could cope in an outdoor environment. By the time Easter came and the threat of snow had gone, we were able to soft release her into an open pen at the back of the pub at Isfield, and from there she would gradually acclimatise back to her natural environment, the wild.

Then it was back on fox patrol when we received an emergency call from workers at the Bexhill brick works. They were concerned about a fox which was bleeding from its face. When we arrived they had managed to trap the fox inside a storage room. The lighting was not good but you could see there was blood on the floor and dripping from the fox's nose, so we had to be careful about how we caught it. We managed to catch him without incurring any further damage to his nose, placed him into a cage and took him out to our ambulance for first aid treatment. Blood was still pouring from his nose and the surrounding fur and whiskers had been burnt. On closer inspection we found that the pads on his feet were also red and burnt.

We dusted trauma powder onto the burns to stop the bleeding, but as it was not a suitable location to apply cooling water we rushed the fox to one of our vets for assessment.

At first I was unsure whether the burns were chemical or heat related, but our vet Chris in Uckfield, assessed the wounds. He was sure they were heat related and was happy with the first aid treatment we'd administered. The fox was placed on antibiotics and pain relief treatment.

We are not sure of the exact cause of the burns but as they were on the fox's feet and nose we thought that he must have ventured inside the brickyard near one of the kilns, or some other heat source, just been a bit too nosy, walked and sniffed at the still hot material and literally got his feet (and his nose) burnt. He was a real character and recovered very well with no complications. We kept him in care for just three weeks, and then took him back to the brickyard and released him at its boundary close to the woodland.

The whole badger, cattle and Tb issue has always been a hot potato and in 2013 the threat of a cull became all too real. WRAS volunteer Kate approached me out of concern, but as WRAS is not a campaigning group, it was difficult for us to do much. However Kate stumbled across a project in the West Country where volunteers were vaccinating badgers against Tb in order to help prevent it spreading and thus trying to avoid a cull.

I encouraged Kate to look into it in more detail which she did with enthusiasm and rigour. The next thing I knew myself and a few other WRAS volunteers had enrolled on the Animal Health and Veterinary Laboratories Agency Badger Cage Trapping and Vaccination training course in Gloucestershire.

The 4-day course was extremely informative. We learnt a lot about bTB and its relationship between badgers and cattle and, more importantly, about the process of badger vaccination and the procedures we need to follow. We had practical hands-on experience of how and where to set traps that involved a very early morning start when we went out and vaccinated 30 badgers and cubs between us. We are delighted and proud to be the first of a team of qualified lay vaccinators available in Sussex to help support the fight against bTB.

In October we were able to announce that farmers in East Sussex could now choose to have the badgers on their land vaccinated against bovine TB. We then set about contacting landowners and drumming up support for vaccination in East Sussex.

Bovine TB (bTB) is a very serious challenge to dairy and beef farmers which can lead to infected cattle being slaughtered and farms being "on shut down" until tested clear of bTB. This causes considerable hardship for the farming community and costs the tax payer a lot of money. Badgers are known to be carriers of bTB and many people believe that the disease can't be controlled solely by improving cattle management.

In the West Country, the government had been carrying out a trial cull of badgers since late August and, if deemed successful, they planned to roll out a badger cull across 40 further areas of England. Part of East Sussex was on the DEFRA "High Risk" list and, as a result, a badger cull could come here as early as June 2014.

The Sussex Badger Vaccination Project was set up as a coalition of East Sussex WRAS, International Animal Rescue and the local Badger Group and believes that badger vaccination is a sustainable approach to reducing bTB in wildlife and cattle without the public opposition associated with badger culling.

We wanted to give farmers in East Sussex an extremely low-cost choice to vaccinate rather than to cull. East Sussex is unique in that geographically it's an "island" of bTB, indeed it has a unique strain of the disease, and therefore is ideal as a test case for a combined approach of badger vaccination and changes in cattle husbandry.

Christmas 2013 ended on a high for WRAS. One of the UK's largest pet insurers, Animal Friends Insurance, decided to celebrate the Christmas festivities by making a huge £70,000 donation to eleven animal charities. We applied and to our huge surprise and delight found ourselves being one of the selected charities.

This could not have come at a better moment as one of our ambulances was old and worn out and come 2014 we would have to take it off the road. With vets bills, food bills, utility bills and other care costs continually increasing we were extremely worried that we wouldn't be able to afford to replace it. This would have left us with a vehicle short and less able to rescue casualties.

The very generous donation of £9,250 from Animal Friends Insurance to sponsor a replacement ambulance has to be the best Christmas Gift our charity has had in years. The concept of a charity Christmas giveaway was the brainwave of Managing Director of Animal Friends Insurance Elaine Fairfax.

Their support has helped us ensure that hundreds of wildlife casualties a year are saved from suffering. Thank you!

The ambulance was a huge asset and within days was on the road and helping to rescue sick and injured animals. It came just in the nick of time as spring 2014 saw a surge in casualties which really stretched us to our limit. Since the beginning of Easter we found ourselves rushed off our feet dealing with an average of twenty five calls for help per day.

Our dedicated Care Team and rescuers worked long hours and on occasions all through the night in order to help Sussex's precious wildlife. Our Care Team were looking after scores of blackbirds, starlings, blue tits, dunnocks, pigeons, doves, ducklings and rabbits.

There were also a number of baby hedgehogs rescued at Firle after their nest was disturbed by a dog and their mum abandoned them; a gosling had to be taken in after getting lost from its parents near Hampden Park; a leucistic starling was rescued after being caught by a cat in Uckfield and six great tit nestlings were brought to WRAS after their nest, inside an air conditioning unit, was disturbed, causing their parents to abandon them.

A hedgehog was picked up having been found wandering around during daylight hours and, using WRAS's ultrasound equipment, was discovered to be pregnant. A young woodpecker was rescued in Battle after being found grounded.

Lindsay, our new Casualty Centre Manager who had taken over from Kate, headed up the Orphan Rearing Team for the first time. I think she was a bit surprised at how busy we became and the volume of calls we started receiving concerning baby birds. There were certainly far more than was normal and even I was surprised. Many of the birds had been picked up by cats and while the wounds from the cats' claws and teeth may appear to be just small punctures, it is quite likely that they will have been infected by bacteria which in turn can cause septicaemia and death. Cats' claws and teeth are laden with lethal bacteria, and while many people think it is shock that kills cat-attacked birds, studies have shown it is usually septicaemia from bacterial infections or hidden internal injuries that kill them.

In 25th June 2014 we had three calls to three fox cubs. The first was late at night and rescuer Tony rushed out to the fox that had been hit by a car. He took it to Highcroft vets in Hailsham for emergency treatment and then to WRAS's centre. The second was another road-casualty cub found near Arlington. This was also seen by emergency vets and then taken to WRAS.

The third cub came from a vets in Burgess Hill. It had been delivered by builders who had rescued it from a septic tank. The fox was covered in human waste and certainly didn't come out smelling of roses! Assistant Manager Chris donned protective clothing and cleaned up the cub under our shower tap.

One of the road casualty foxes had pelvic damage and the other had rib damage. Neither was able to stand properly when admitted. We continued

188

their care at our Casualty Centre and slowly they all improved and regained their use of their legs. To our surprise they all made a full recovery and were released back to where found.

Our dedicated Care Team work long hours on call for emergencies and deal with the care of animals already in WRAS's Centre. It's not uncommon for us to work through the whole day and before we know it we are working into the night. Most days our small staff work more hours than they are paid for, and the volunteers put in extra time as well. None of us would do it if we didn't love it and care so much for the animals in our protection.

Sadly not all casualties make it despite all the hard work our Care Team and the vets put into trying to save them. To lose a casualty, having spent weeks caring for them and giving the medication a chance to work, can be very upsetting. We try hard not to get attached to an animal, but they can be so endearing and helpless, that we have all ended up having a cry from time to time. The worst heart ache occurs with the babies. We have had several young animals admitted from time to time and you are up every few hours feeding them, day after day after day. Your lack of sleep starts to cloud your emotional ability to keep detached, and if one dies it can be a real wrench to the system. Several people have been on the receiving end of an emotional outburst after being up all night for ages or you've been struggling to stay on top of a casualty's condition. Even out on rescues, if you are dealing with a long winded situation and you have been giving it your all, and at the end of it the casualties dies or has to be put to sleep, its very hard. In front of the public you stay professional but its when the adrenaline wares off it hits you hard. You have to find a way to cope and find a release for your emotion or it will eat you up and destroy you.

WRAS is funded by volunteers and donations from the public and relies on this funding to keep the service running across East Sussex. From the early days when I had to jump on the bus to get to a rescue, to forming WRAS and then getting our first ambulance, or first Casualty Centre, first vet and first member of staff, it amazes me the way the organisation has grown and developed.

189

The charity now receives between 2-3,000 calls for help every year, and struggles to cope with the workload which can be as high as 110 calls in a day. WRAS has expanded and improved its facilities again and again, trying to help as many people as possible and the casualties they find. It's really heart-warming when I meet people who tell me what a great job we are doing and reach into their pockets and give a donation to help support our work. These people really lift us when we are down after losing a casualty.

I know we are not able to help everyone but we try our best to help as many as possible. I wish we could do more, but we need to ensure that the casualties we are able to take in are properly looked after and cared for, always working closely with our veterinary team.

What's the best part? It's the chance to release casualties back to the wild; being able to see all our hard work paying off and leading to the release of a sick animal back to its natural environment. It may only be a few seconds; a sparrow flying out of a pod, or thirty seconds; a hedgehog uncurling and dashing behind some bushes, but we get such joy from seeing their faces as they sniff the air and recognise familiar surroundings. They might not stop to say thank you and they might not realise that we have helped them or even saved their life, but we do know they are glad to be home and back where they belong. It does the soul good!

Unlike their domestic and agricultural cousins, wildlife does not have owners to look after them. They don't have furry purses to pay for their vets' bills, but they do have WRAS.

Chapter 19 – I'm getting old!

In August 2014 we were finally able to make a start on vaccinating badgers, the first ever to be vaccinated against bTB in Sussex. Our first sites were both in Uckfield; one at the Sussex Horse Rescue Centre and the other in Kathy's back garden, which happens to be very close to the back of the horse rescue centre.

The process of vaccination takes just over two weeks. The first week is spent pre-baiting and encouraging badgers to forage for food in set areas by putting down one of their favourite foods - peanuts. The second week we move the traps onto the site and encourage the badgers to feed in them - again enticed by peanuts. Once the badgers feel safe the traps they are wired up ready to catch any that should enter. The cages are quite large and have a mechanism that trips the gate shut when a badger moves the trigger inside. At first light we check the traps and any badgers that have been caught are vaccinated. We do this by injecting them through the cage mesh. They are then released to go back to their family. The vaccine doesn't cure a badger with TB, but does protect badgers against catching TB. As a result the vaccination work takes place over a minimum of four years so that as those with TB die out the surviving badgers are TB free. The aim is not to vaccination all the badgers and scientific studies have shown that herd immunity sufficient after four years with a coverage of approximately 80% of the local population significantly reduces the ability of TB to spread.

The Horse Sanctuary was a difficult site as there were no main setts but a lot of foraging taking place, and potentially two or three social groups entering different parts of the farm. The area closest to the town was particularly problematic which was why we decided to add Kathy's garden onto the licence, believing that the two badgers that frequented her garden were the same badgers that were visiting the town side of the farm.

Normally we set the traps in the late afternoon and return to check them at first light, but at Kathy's we were able to sit indoors and monitor the situation from the comfort of her living room. So as soon as we spotted a badger entering the trap we were able to go out, vaccinate and release there and then. The first badger was entrapped within a couple of hours, and to our surprise just before midnight a second badger was also caught and vaccinated.

Pleased with our first success, the following morning we were up before the lark to check the traps up at the farm. Unfortunately the weather had turned. It was a lot wetter than expected. WRAS's new vet Mike, along with Kathy, Chris and I met at the farm at 5am and by 5.30am we were marching across the fields to find out how successful we had been. The first traps were all closed with no badgers inside. We moved to the next site; they too were all closed. By now we were very worried as to why the traps had shut and no badger inside. We moved up the hill to the next site and our hearts lifted when we saw a trap containing a badger. From a distance we donned the necessary gear; waterproof clothing, face masks, face shields, gloves and wellington boots. We approached as quietly as possible armed with the vaccine, a marker spray and scissors. This badger was quite easy to inject. We then cut a small patch of guard hairs and sprayed it so it could be easily identified if caught the second night. There was no point in giving him a double dose of vaccine.

With our spirits raised, we moved on to the final area and the last five traps, but they started to waver as one after another the traps had again closed, but were empty. Until, in the last trap, there was another badger.

Rather disappointed that we hadn't caught more, we sat down and thought about the day's events and why so many of our traps had been tripped but were empty. We decided to call Woodchester Park in Gloucestershire; a scientific study centre that has been long involved in monitoring badger vaccination and leading the development of the Badger Vaccination Programme. They were certain that we had set the traps without enough slack in the string and the wet weather had caused the string to tighten and trip the traps before the badgers had a chance to enter.

Vaccination is carried out over two consecutive nights so having reset the traps with slacker string, allowing for the wet weather, at first light the following day we were back again. This time we had managed to trap two more, un-vaccinated badgers. Although the other traps had not been tripped, they still had food in them indicating that we had actually caught all or most of the visiting badgers. An encouragingly positive outcome!

This was a huge learning curve and set us on a good footing for future vaccinations.

After discussions with DEFRA and various other bodies it was apparent we would be able to apply for various grant funding to help with vaccination work. The stakeholder group which we had helped form was made up of various local organisations or individuals with an interest in fighting bTB in Sussex. We were all in agreement that we should target the High Risk area of East Sussex.

Having received a legacy, WRAS was in the fortunate position to be able to employ Chris Riddington, our weekend manager, to work full time for WRAS for 12 months with a remit to help support the Sussex Badger Vaccination Project. This was in addition to his work as manager and we hoped that grant funding would eventually allow the Vaccination Project to employ him direct.

After a number of meetings and presentations with landowners, farmers and councils the project managed to get expressions of interest from landowners covering 120 square kilometres of East Sussex. The potentially most nerve racking was the meeting with "The Ruminators", a group of Sussex cattle farmers at the Ardingly Showground.   I attended with Kate Edmonds, one of the other directors of Sussex Badger Vaccination Project. Knowing how anti-vaccination some farmers can be we tried to balance our presentation and keep it factual. We were certainly challenged with some hard questions but Kate and I coped better than even we expected. We were amazed that by the end almost everyone in the room was interested in undertaking vaccination on their land.   To our delight and surprise we received a round of applause and thanks for our presentation. I truly hope this is the start of things to come and that the badger vaccination project goes from strength to strength.

On September 9th I received a very worrying phone call from the Swan Sanctuary at Shepperton. Staff from Eastbourne Borough Council had found a dead cygnet at Decoy Pond in Hampden Park and asked specialist veterinary staff at the Swan Sanctuary to carry out a post mortem. They were shocked at the cygnet's condition. He weighed just 2.7kg, almost half its expected weight, due to a severe parasite burden.

This was the first time cygnets had hatched at this pond since 2008 when several of the previous family had also been found dead and resulted in us rescuing the remaining members of the swan family and taking them to the safety of the Swan Sanctuary. It was clear we were about to have the same problem and needed to act fast.

We took our walk-on-scales down to the park to check the weight of the cygnets hoping that the one which had died was a runt and more susceptible to illness. Luckily mum, dad and three of the five remaining cygnets were on the grass, so Kathy and I managed to catch two of the youngsters and weigh them. They were about 3.9kg and 3.2kg, quite a bit lower than we would have expected.

We phoned the Swan Sanctuary's vet nurse, Mel Beeson, to talk over the cygnets' condition and a decision was taken to catch the three remaining cygnets and try to check one of the parent's weight too.

It was clear the cygnets were nowhere near as lively as they should be, so we decided to go for the slow and patient approach waiting for suitable opportunities to catch them and the parents where possible. Our second capture saw another cygnet and also dad caught. The cygnet was only 3.1kg but dad was a good 12kg weight. Volunteer Rescuer Tony collected these four and took them to WRAS's Casualty Centre at Whitesmith, whilst Kathy and I set about catching the remaining two cygnets.

Using an inflatable boat I went out onto the lake to try and find them. I spotted one at the far side near the bank, so backed off giving Kathy enough time and space to catch it from land. The poor little chap didn't put up much fight at all, was not interested in food but was drinking a lot. We weighed this one which was 2.9kg.

The last cygnet was found by the inlet stream and slowly floating closer to the bank and I caught him with a long handled net. He had no fight in him either and weighed just 2.6kg. These last two cygnets were very worrying and clearly not very strong, so after seeking advice from the Swan Sanctuary it was decided to take them up to their hospital as a matter of urgency. We were hoping to bring both parents in to be with their young but mum was proving difficult to catch, and as the cygnets were so poorly and dad was clearly in good condition, it was decided to release him back with his partner to keep her company. The cygnets would keep each other company and were going to need a lot of love and care from the staff at the Swan Sanctuary.

Three of the five cygnets proved to be so poorly that veterinary staff at the Swan Sanctuary had to place them on intravenous fluids. The other two were more lively, a better weight and showing signs of starting to eat for themselves. The cygnets all remained in a critical condition and remained in the intensive care for the first 3 days. Sadly one of them died, but the remaining four have done very well, but are staying at the Swan Sanctuary and it is hoped that once old enough they may return to Sussex.

October 2014 saw us release a buzzard back in its home range along the Broyle at Ringmer.

The Buzzard is one the county's biggest birds of prey. On October 20th at 11pm a passing motorist spotted one at the side of the B2192, The Broyle, between Ringmer and Halland almost outside the Raystede Centre for Animal Welfare, but sadly they don't operate out of hours. Chris, who was on call that night, went to attend to the buzzard which was very dazed and concussed.

Under veterinary advice, Chris gave the bird emergency medication and cleaned up a would on its chest. The following morning the Buzzard was seen at Henley House Vets in Uckfield where the wound received further treatment and suturing.

We had dealt with nine buzzards over the previous five years and all of them had old fractures and internal injuries and had to be put to sleep. We had even transported them to other rescue centres elsewhere in the country for specialist veterinary advice and support, but despite best efforts, all had to be euthanized. This was been very disheartening.

The Broyle buzzard remained very concussed and dazed for most of the week and the outcome did not look good. But then, over the weekend, he came round, started to perk up and became much livelier. We moved him to one of our large indoor pen so he could spread his wings and fly. We were all delighted to see him recover so well and walked round with smiles on our faces for ages.

One week later the buzzard was taken back to The Broyle and released back into his home range and back to the wild. We were so happy to see him go. This is what we strive to achieve with all the casualties that come into our care. We really weren't sure whether he was going to recover and are really pleased for him. Another example of the vital work our out-of-hour rescue service provides.

In November we received a visit from BBC One's Countryfile. They spent the filming day with WRAS's new vet Mike Symons, as well as with our hard working Feed & Clean Shift volunteers and managers Lindsay and Kathy. It was a very quiet day on the rescue front but suddenly late in the day there came a call about a deer in difficulty near Battle.

Countryfile presenter Joe Crowley, better known for his reports on the BBC's One Show, jumped on board our ambulance to come with us for the rescue. We found the deer, an adult fallow buck with full palmate antlers, thrashing around violently having been caught in a rope fence in the middle of a field. Chris and Kathy arrived shortly after us. I cautiously approached to assess the situation as it was not clear how, and to what extent, the deer had been caught. It was not going to be an easy rescue. Kathy and I approached hoping to capture the deer using a walk-to-wards net, but it didn't quite go according to plan. As I tried to secure the deer it moved and my legs were at risk of being kicked. I managed to roll forwards and gain control of the deer, allowing Chris and Kathy to start cutting the rope. Luckily most of the rope was going between the two antlers making our job of cutting it away much easier.

With the rope and rescue net removed it was time for Kathy and Chris to moved away, leaving me with the job of releasing the deer. I found myself in an awkward position and would have to get up and move away quickly to avoid being kicked or stabbed by the antlers. I took a deep breath and sprang backwards as swiftly as I was able. It worked! Which was just as well as we were being filmed. We were relieved to see the deer spring to his feet and run off across the field to freedom. The programme was aired on 7th December and it was some of the most dramatic footage of a deer rescue I've ever seen. I don't think I realised quite how close I had been to being seriously injured.

Our Casualty Centre Management now consisted of myself as the Operations Director, Lindsay Redfern, Kathy Martyn and Chris Riddington as Centre Managers and Kirsti Sibbald as Assistant Manager. Kathy was still working voluntarily but the rest of us were on minimum wage for 34 hours a week, but as always working quite a lot more than this – in fact there have been times when we have worked up to 110 hours a week each. Our team is now the best it has ever been. For the first time in over six years Kathy and I managed to take several days off including Christmas Day. For the first time ever I didn't even have to answer the rescue line too!

January 2015 started with a few unusual calls. The first saw Chris, Tony and I rushing out to a report of a swan covered in blood on the Pevensey Levels. I've never seen anything quite like it. The swan was completely red; no white feathers at all, just blood everywhere.

Our efforts were hampered due to flooding across the field. On our first attempt at capture the swan managed to take off. We were really surprised that she was able to fly but as it was so windy it really didn't take much more than the swan opening it wings in order to take off. It was an extraordinary sight. A flying red swan!

She landed in a drainage dyke at the far side of the field. To get there we had one large dyke and three smaller dykes to cross. The first three channels, normally dry during the summer, were about knee deep in water. The swan had certainly found an awkward place for me to get to but an ideal place to try and capture her. Having waded through the first three smaller dykes there was only one thing for it; to take off my jacket and fleece and swim across the large dyke.

The plan worked and I successfully managed to catch the swan. I was a bit worried about how I was going to get her back across the dyke; I didn't really fancy swimming with her tucked under my arm. But with Chris's help we managed to manoeuvre her back across the dyke and to WRAS's ambulance. I was soaking wet from head to toe and very cold. So after bedding down the swan and providing first aid, Chris wrapped a blanket round me and drove the pair of us, one bloody and one wet, back to WRAS's Casualty Centre for treatment and a hot drink respectively.

The swan was found to have numerous deep cuts, one of which was a venus bleed from her beak. We applied a trauma gauze to the lower beak to help stop the bleeding and taped it in place. After seeking advice from the Swan Sanctuary's Veterinary Team we decided to send her up to their specialist vets to assess. I'm glad we did. These experts even had problems and ended up calling their vet out during the night.

After ten days in care what was a bright red, blood-covered swan turned back into a beautiful white swan.

We are still not sure exactly what caused the injuries but it is possible the swan may have hit overhead cables or crash landed into bushes or fencing. As the swan preened to clean up the blood, it had the effect of spreading it all over her body and so turning herself red.

On the 19th January the swan was returned back to Sussex. Chris and I took her back to Wartling on the Pevensey Levels and released her, hopefully to be reunited with her partner. The swan was clearly excited when we got out the ambulance. She was looking round and you could just tell she knew where she was and was home again.

We released her into the small channel of water where originally rescued. We watched her from a distance for a while. We were delighted to see her take off, fly round the field gaining height and then off she flew in a westerly direction. I suspect these fields were not the swans' home but the pair had landed there when she was injured. They probably have a location nearby to which they were returning for breeding this spring, and she will head there hopefully to find her mate.

This is one of the main reasons why we undertake this work; it is such a buzz being able to return such magnificent creatures back to the wild. It was a great outcome for us, thanks to the hard work of the staff at the Swan Sanctuary at Shepperton and our volunteers at East Sussex WRAS.

The next strange and rather shocking incident occurred near Ringmer. A tawny owl had been hit by a car on the Broyle and was on the ground unable to fly. A passing motorist had spotted the bird and not knowing what to do, he had decided his best course of action was to put it out of its misery. So the well-meaning, but misguided gentleman had placed the owl on the road and then run over it, repeatedly. This was the only way he could think of killing it and ending its suffering.

When I arrived he was still sitting in his car with his hazard lights flashing and explained what he had done. Although I applaud this gentleman for stopping rather than just driving on, repeatedly running over a casualty to end its suffering is not a suitable way to end life and can cause even greater suffering. He was unable to describe the bird's injuries and did not know the bird's full condition but assumed that if it had been hit by a car it would need putting down.

I diplomatically told him that in the future he should call us, or a vets, and he was surprised that vets would be interested in dealing with wildlife and also concerned about the costs involved. I explained that if a casualty is suffering and needs putting to sleep all good quality veterinary practices will do so free of charge, or if treatable they will hold onto the casualty and pass it on to wildlife organisations like WRAS.

We deal with hundreds of road casualty calls each year and they range from small mammals like hedgehogs to larger animals like swans and badgers. Many are fatally injured by vehicles but many are merely concussed and can be treated.

Very rarely does a casualty need putting to sleep on the roadside. We wouldn't advise motorists to attempt to pick up foxes, badgers, swans and similar wildlife which can be hazardous but to call a rescue organisation for assistance.

I would also urge motorists not to move a casualty unless they have to for safety reasons; for either that of the casualty or other motorists to avoid potential additional injuries. The best advice is to either cover the animal with a towel if safe to approach, and if by doing so you are not going to encourage it to move or run out into traffic and more danger. Otherwise keep back, observe from a distance and call for help.

This incident got a lot of publicity so we really hope we have helped save many more wild animals and birds from suffering.

In February WRAS rescuers Chris and Keith were called to help a rook caught high up in a tree in Lewes. Upon arrival they quickly spotted the bird and assessed the scene for access points by which they might be able to try and reach the casualty. The bird was in quite a bad way and in obvious discomfort; he was caught upside down between two branches and desperately flapping his wings in a vain attempt to free himself. It swiftly became clear that our ladders wouldn't reach, so a call was made to East Sussex Fire and Rescue Service for assistance.

The fire service arrived within minutes and after talking through the options they decided on health and safety grounds they would have to call in the larger turn-table engine from Brighton. The road was closed off and WRAS helped divert traffic around the area and the fire service got to work. Two firefighters went up in the cage and with some skilful manoeuvring managed to drop down on top of the rook and free it from the branch and bring it down to the awaiting rescuers below.

The bird was given the once over in the ambulance and then rushed to WRAS's casualty centre in Whitesmith. Lindsay and I checked the rook on arrival, warmed him up gently and wrapped him in an insulating and absorbent blanket and gave him much needed fluids and medication.

After several days of rest and recuperation the rook was suitable for release and was taken back to Lewes to fly off back to his or her rookery.

February also saw an encounter with a Brown Long Eared Bat at Piltdown near Uckfield. The finder had found the bat after it was caught by their cat and had left the injured bat hanging from a bird feeder for three days.

Eventually the finder called us, and Chris and I carefully picked the bat off the feeder and gently warmed him up before giving vital life-saving fluids.

There was clearly a wound on the bat's chest as well as puncture marks on the wings, most likely all inflicted by the cat. Cats can have extremely poisonous claws and we took it to the woman who knows more about bats than probably anyone, Jenny Clark MBE , and her Bat Hospital at Forest Row for medication and treatment.

April saw WRAS reach the finals of the 2015 CEVA Animal Welfare Awards Charity Team of the Year. This was a prestigious event with hundreds of nominations . We had reached the final three! Kathy, Chris, Vet Simon, volunteers Sally and Jeanette as well as myself attended the ceremony at the Grand Burlington Hotel in the centre of Birmingham. WRAS was up against some tough competition. We didn't win, but to have got so far in such a highly esteemed veterinary award event was amazing. I feel so proud of the work that our small charity is able to carry out, and especially of all the hard work that our volunteers dedicatedly do, day in day out – and all on a voluntary basis. There are truly some amazing people

out there working hard for animal welfare. While we might not have won the award we did win the charity raffle and came away with a hotel stay worth £250, a framed certificate and a personalised crystal pyramid saying "CEVA Charity Team of the Year Finalist."

On a less happy, and indeed a very distressing note, shortly after this we encountered a hedgehog theft. WRAS had been looking after 95 hedgehogs over the winter and was in the joyful process of returning them all to their home ranges. Some are kept at the centre, others are in secure pens with various volunteers with appropriate facilities. Then we discovered two of them, "Swimmer" and "Cherry" were missing and there was no way they could have escaped. We hunted high and low doubting that they had gone. Eventually we came to the sad conclusion that they must have been taken. We believe it must have happened at some point between 8pm Friday 17th April and 11am Saturday 18th April. The pens and hedgehogs are checked twice a day and this missing pair were about to be put into carriers, returned to our Casualty Centre and taken out for release.

The two hedgehogs had been microchipped and can be identified. WRAS appealed for the hedgehogs to be returned as wild hedgehogs do not make good pets and struggle to survive if released into an area which does not already have hedgehogs.

Our volunteers had worked so hard over winter looking after these hedgehogs and it feels like a kick in the teeth that someone had taken them and wasted all our hard work. More crucially we obviously don't want them to end up suffering. This is the first time we have had anything like this happen. Sussex Police were informed and we found out that the same evening some pet rabbits had been stolen from a garden. We still hope they may return.

The two hedgehogs taken were "Swimmer" a female Hedgehog admitted into WRAS's Care on 2nd October 2014. She was found fallen into swimming pool in Upper Dicker weighing 368grams. She was very chesty as a result of taking in water, and needed closed observation, a diuretic, antibiotics and worming.

The other hedgehog take was "Cherry" another female Hedgehog admitted into WRAS's Care on 2nd November 2014. Found out during the day time in a garden in Heathfield weighing 290grams. This hedgehog was found out in the day time in the middle of a garden, with no obvious injuries, but way too small to survive hibernation. The hedgehog had to be treated for Lungworm and Roundworm burdens.

It kept going through our minds; why would someone would do this? It just doesn't make sense. Their pen doors were securely shut and clever though they may be, they could not have escaped by themselves. We have now put padlocks on all our pens and enclosures at various sites across the county.

After this disappointing and sad event, spirits were lifted when we were called to an unusual hedgehog rescue with a successful outcome.

A lady phoned WRAS having struggled to find anyone to help her. She told us that she normally fed two hedgehogs in her garden but noticed that one was missing. She then discovered that one of her neighbours had found a hedgehog in their basement patio garden. It had fallen down the embankment and wall and had become stuck and unable to get out of the small area below.

Well nothing too unusual there you might say. The problem was the hedgehog had taken up residence in a drainage pipe that went into the retaining wall. Each time the residents tried to catch the hedgehog it would run to the pipe and climb back inside.

Kathy and I decided there was only one thing for it; to sit up, wait for it to come out of the pipe and then block its escape.

There was quite a bit of dust, dirt and rubble that the hedgehog had managed to dig out from the end of the pipe and deposit on the patio. It was as if she was trying to burrow her way to freedom along the pipe. It would have been impossible for the hedgehog to get out via the patio basement as the surrounding wall was over 5ft tall. The residents had put out water and cat food to help sustain the hedgehog but were desperate for someone to save their prickly lodger.

I helped Kathy climb up onto the top of the wall and then climbed up myself. It was not exactly warm, so we got ourselves a little picnic of food and coffee and positioned ourselves so we could drop a net down blocking the pipe once the hedgehog was out.

We used a children's night vision scope to watch for the hedgehog. We could hear her inside the pipe as she munched on a small piece of cat food that we had placed inside it to encourage her out. She coughed a few times, which worried us as it sounded very much like a lung worm parasite cough. So we did not want to give up on her, and very much felt we had to rescue her to save her life.

Over an hour later we saw the hedgehog for the first time as she poked her head out of the pipe and sniffed round. We had placed a couple of bits of food slightly further away from the pipe and then a dish of food even further away. As hedgehogs can run quite fast, we wanted to make sure she was far enough away from the pipe so that we could drop a net down to cover the pipe entrance to block off her hidey-hole.

Using the night scope Kathy whispered instructions to me. Eventually the hedgehog moved away from the hole to the dish, giving the perfect opportunity to spring into action. As soon as the pipe was blocked, Kathy jumped down off the wall to pick up the hedgehog.

Once in the light of the flat, we were able to check her over and noticed how short her toe nails were from all the determined, yet hopeless, digging. What could have been a heart-breaking out-come, was now a very satisfactory rescue and we took her back to the safe haven of WRAS's Casualty Care Centre at Whitesmith.

To our surprise, we discovered that this hedgehog had the remains of white Tipex marks on her spines, a method we have previously used to mark hedgehogs whilst in care. So we are sure this is one which has been in care with WRAS before.

This was certainly an unusual rescue. It might not have been the most dramatic of rescues, but our legs ached from sitting so still and for so long on top of the wall. And not on the warmest of evenings! But had we not done so she would have been stuck for ages and most likely died of exhaustion after so much desperate digging. I am so glad we rescued her and she is now safe.

Education is key, and as part of our celebrations in 2015, WRAS purchased an educational trailer, which is in the process of being constructed. This has been funded by generous donations to help with this project. We hope that as part of our 30th year celebrations we will be able to visit various schools, colleges and community groups as well as public events. Our aim is to increase awareness of the work of WRAS; to educate and inform people how they can best deal with any injured animals they come across and along the way we hope this may help reduce some of the casualties we rescue, treat and ideally release back to the wild on a daily basis.

Thanks to the legacy we received the previous year we have found ourselves in a position where we can finish off the work at WRAS Casualty Centre. We were rather behind with our original five to six year plan so this is a big relief. Over the past year Bruce, our landlord, has been busy replacing the roof, resurfacing the area around the building and improving the site. Our volunteer, education and cold rooms were only temporary, but now we have been offered the neighbouring unit as a permanent home. The overall area is slightly smaller but it's a much better space. So with the help of our vets, staff and volunteers we have designed the new units with better use of space. We have replaced some of the older facilities and with the benefit of hindsight, experience and expert advice the centre is emerging improved and transformed.

We are in the process of equipping the new theatre, reception, assessment room, additional prep areas, orphan rearing room, extra indoor pens and volunteer room, kitchen, toilet and shower, plus storage and office. We owe Bruce, our landlord, Andy his site manager and builder and Tim our carpenter and joiner a huge amount of gratitude for all they have done to help and support us as WRAS goes from strength to strength.

2015 saw me start my thirtieth year in this animal rescue business. Where will I be in another thirty years? Probably in a coffin the way I am going, though I hope not.

WRAS now received over 2500 calls for help a year, takes in up to 250 casualties at a time, has three full time and two part time members of staff who work minimum wage, three registered vets, four veterinary ambulances and over 100 volunteers. This has changed so much since I started on my own 30 years ago. I am so proud of all our volunteers and staff and I'm amazed at how they cope when we are so busy.

Chris and I now take turns in having the rescue line one week on one week off, although it is nice to have someone who realises how stressful and exhausting it is doing it 24 hours a day.

We are not a large rich charity and we rely on donation, and it is a constant worry where the funding is coming from all the time to pay the bills. Our biggest income is regular monthly donations via bank standing orders, without these kind people WRAS would really struggle.

My dream is for WRAS to be in a position where it never has to worry about whether it can afford to take in a casualty, or have enough space, volunteers or staff.

Whether you are local to East Sussex or miles away, please support your local wildlife rescue or hospital. They are some of the most under-funded and under-valued people and organisations in the country.

Animals don't have much and they will fight tooth and claw to keep that valuable life, it's our job to help them do that.

Thank you.

East Sussex Wildlife Rescue & Ambulance Service (WRAS) is a registered Charity number 1108880 and helps thousands of wildlife casualties every year. The charity is funded purely by donations, standing orders, occasional grants, and by people leaving legacies.

From small baby birds to seals and deer East Sussex WRAS helps as many people and wildlife casualties as they can and relieves their suffering.

Please support their vital lifesaving work by making a one off donation, a regular monthly donation or by leaving WRAS a gift if in will.

Donations can be sent to East Sussex WRAS, PO Box 2148, Seaford, East Sussex, BN25 9DE or online at www.wildlifeambulance.org as well as over the phone by calling 01825-873003.

Thank you.